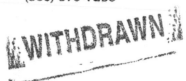

RANDOM ACTS OF GRACE

RANDOM ACTS OF GRACE

Dramatic
Encounters
with God's
Love

Paul & Nicole Johnson

Moorings
Nashville, Tennessee
A Division of The Ballantine Publishing Group,
Random House, Inc.

RANDOM ACTS OF GRACE

Scripture quotations noted NKJV are from THE NEW KING JAMES VERSION. Copyright © 1979, 1980, 1982, Thomas Nelson, Inc., Publishers.

Life of the Beloved: Spiritual Living in a Secular World by Henri J. M. Nouwen. Copyright © 1992 by Henri J. M. Nouwen. Reprinted by permission of The CROSSROAD Publishing Co., New York.

ISBN: 0-345-39752-5

Library of Congress Catalog Card Number : 95-078309

First Edition: September 1995

10 9 8 7 6 5 4 3 2 1

CONTENTS

PART FOUR: LIVING FREE

ACKNOWLEDGMENTS

There are generally three categories of "thank-yous":

The thank-you-for-loving-us-and-believing-in-us category: To all of our family, our friends, and all of those that have booked us, attended our shows, prayed for us, and bought our resources. And to our veterinarians, Lisa and Wayne.

The thank-you-for-your-continual-hard-work-on-our-behalf category: To the Moorings staff; Brian Dominey, Audrey Adams, Denise George, Angela Guffey, Ken Cope, Martin Culpepper, Cheryl Richards, and Robert Smith.

The there's-no-way-on-God's-green-earth-that-we-could-ever-have-done-this-without-you category: To Mike and Gail Hyatt, and Robert and Bobbie Wolgemuth.

FOREWORD

Random Acts of Grace is an encouraging and up-lifting journey through the ordinariness of our daily lives into the extraordinariness of God's love. Each story is filled with the familiar clutter and ambiguity of everyday life where God always seems ready to surprise us with his inexhaustible grace.

These are not the stories of some faraway fantasy. These are the stories of our humanity, the stories of mistakes and flaws and misunderstandings, which, because of Jesus, can also be the stories of hope and forgiveness and healing.

Sometimes it feels as though God is hiding from us when we are in the midst of pain or loneliness or depression. Through this book of stories, Paul and Nicole Johnson help us see that God is not hiding *from* our pain; he is hiding *in* our pain, if we'll just look.

—Mike Yaconelli
Senior Editor, *The Door*
Co-Founder, Youth Specialties

INTRODUCTION

Stories impact our lives. Whether it be the tale told at dinner about something that happened at the grocery store, or the bedtime story that comforts our children as they close their eyes to sleep, we are a people of story. And we come by that love of stories from God. He has told us how he created the world, and how he made us, and he has told us stories of his great love for us. He demonstrated that love by bringing those stories to life. And when Jesus walked on the earth, he, too, told stories—stories of love and forgiveness, of bitterness and anger, of healing and hope.

Random Acts of Grace is a collection of such stories. Some of these stories are cries of the heart, some are confessions of the soul, and others are simple life experiences. All of them are fictional, but all are, in some way, about God's grace, his unmerited favor and love toward us in Christ. God does not love us *because* we are a certain way. His love is not a reward for good behavior. God's love is not like any other love we have ever known. Whenever or however we find it, God's grace surprises us, catches us unaware, challenges us, and sometimes offends us.

This book is about encountering God's overwhelming grace and love in the mundane and the sometimes dramatic moments of life. The characters in this book catch a glimpse of the divine love for which their hearts long. They do not grasp it all at one time, but piece by piece, or glimpse by glimpse, as he reveals it to them, through random acts of grace.

Is God's grace really random? *Random* means lacking a definite pattern or purpose. And God definitely has a pattern and a purpose. But consider that if we do not know the purpose, or if the pattern is too large to comprehend, then the way his grace and love intersect our lives rarely seems more than random. We are left to experience God's grace spontaneously and unexpectantly.

And *spontaneous* describes what happened in February of 1988: We started a traveling theater show. Convinced that we could communicate the gospel through stories, we began writing short comedic/dramatic sketches. We performed these pieces anywhere and everywhere that people would have us. We had no idea when we started this work that God would use it in the way that he has. Quite a random act of grace. We have performed in more than two thousand settings for more than a half a million people!

As actors, married to each other, and on the road constantly, we have had some . . . interesting times. Our writing reflects this fact. While none of these stories is autobiographical, all of these stories have roots in our journeys of faith. From "The Lost Key" to "Baby," we have laughed, cried, struggled, and learned more about the love of God than we ever imagined possible. Another random act of grace. And there is still so much more to learn.

When we read stories as children, we felt as though we met new people. Even today, we are always sad to see a book come to an end, and we almost always find ourselves missing the characters. That is also true for writing a book. You spend a lot of time with your own "people" when you are writing their words, creating their situations and watching them wrestle with their faith. You also learn a lot. So when it is over, and you turn in a finished book, you find a big part of your life is missing. We became so involved with these characters that now that this work is completed, it almost feels like they have moved.

In a way, they *did* move. They moved from our neighborhood to yours. So get to know these new "people" who now live next door to you, share an office with you, or go to the same store or church as you do. In some cases you may see yourself. Although their stories are gathered in this book in almost random fashion, these characters have a lot to teach us. They come by their wisdom from real life, each of them at a different point in their journey of faith. Some of them desperate for God's grace; others quite resistant. Either way they have impacted our lives forever. And maybe when you close the book, and these people move on, you, too, will find yourself missing them.

PART ONE

FACING TRUTH

"But he has got nothing on," said a little child. . . .

The Emperor writhed, for he knew it was true. But he thought, "The procession must go on now." So he held himself stiffer than ever, and the chamberlains held up the invisible train.

—Hans Christian Andersen,
The Emperor's New Clothes

"You shall know the truth, and the truth shall make you free."

—Jesus Christ (John 8:32 NKJV)

The higher our level of pretending, the farther we have to fall. How could we face what is really true without grace? Read on to enter into the lives of several characters struggling to find the grace to admit what is true about themselves.

The Lost Key

When I walked in the front door after the longest day of my life, there were people in my living room. Not just any people, but our friends the Joneses. The proverbial couple that we were "trying to keep up with." *What are they doing here?*

I caught my wife's icy stare about the time I remembered. Tuesday night, six o'clock, Matt and Terry. *Stupid, stupid, stupid,* I thought to myself. I could tell my thoughts were being read, like a cartoon balloon over my head.

"I'm sorry I'm late," I offered lamely.

"Change your clothes and join us," Beth said flatly, trying to be civil. I held her glare for a moment. Maybe a watched pot would not boil.

No such luck. She had a thousand questions and they were steaming out her ears.

We made it through dinner. Beth would not look at me. Luckily for me, we didn't know Matt and Terry well enough for them to detect anything unusual. Our conversation was superficial, but, then again, it always is. We had dessert and coffee, and then Matt started looking at his watch. We went through the pre-parting phrases: "It's getting late," and, "Yeah, I guess we'd better get the kids." Of course it was only eight-thirty, but what else do you say? I secretly wanted the Joneses to stay all night in hopes of defusing my wife's anger, but I was simply delaying the inevitable.

"I'll walk you out." It would give me a chance to apologize again. *How had I forgotten that they were coming over? Oh, well, just one of those things.* "Thanks again for coming," I said at the car.

"Thanks for inviting us. We had a great time," Terry said. "Next time, we'll have you guys over." She seemed sincere enough.

"I'll go in right now and tie a ribbon around my neck."

Matt waved away my apology. "Don't think twice about it, Bill. No big deal." I momentarily imagined Beth being as forgiving as Matt Jones. I liked him more every minute.

"Thanks. Good night." I waved, and sighed. Then I headed for the kitchen to make peace with my wife. But I was not prepared for what followed.

Beth was in the kitchen putting away the food. I ran the sink full of hot dishwater and assumed my normal position. As I washed, I didn't just *sense* she was angry; I felt her anger radiating throughout the room. *What is the big deal? So I forgot we were having company. If she knew what kind of day I've had.*

My thoughts were interrupted by the slamming down of the silverware she was putting away. I continued washing, pretending to be oblivious to her actions, while I planned my strategy. *Surely it isn't just the dinner she's mad about.* I decided to go for the old standby: "Dinner was great."

Silence.

"Honey, what's wrong?"

Silence.

"Honey? Talk to me. What's wrong?"

"Nothing." More slamming.

"Now I know that when you say, 'Nothing,' your 'Nothing' definitely means *something.*"

Silence. As cold as marble.

"Are you mad at me about being late?" I ventured. Better to get her talking than continue to let the tension steep. It seemed strong enough already.

"I'm not mad!" she practically yelled. Realizing the inconsistency in her words and actions, she settled down a little. "I'm disappointed."

"Aw, honey, come on. I just forgot."

"That's what you always say."

"I said I was sorry."

"I'm sure you are!"

I saw the fire in her eyes and felt my own anger welling up inside my chest. "What's that supposed to mean?" I demanded.

"It's just that you say 'I'm sorry' all the time, but you consistently forget things, and I don't see you making any effort to remember."

"I remember things. Do you think I'd have a job if I couldn't remember anything? Do you think we'd be in the house we're in if I couldn't remember anything?"

"I exaggerated," she said. "It's the *little* things."

"Like what?"

"Like two weeks ago, when you were going to pick up Katie from Mother's Day Out. Or two days ago, when you promised to stop by the grocery on your way home. Or yesterday, when you were supposed to call your sister about the lawn mower in the garage. . . ."

"Okay. . . ."

"Or tonight when the Joneses had been in our house for one solid hour before you remembered we were having company and decided to come home."

"Okay! Stop it."

"Bill, why can't you remember?"

"Well, maybe if you didn't get so mad at me, I could remember!" I was enraged. Didn't she see how demeaning her attitude was toward me?

"I'm not mad."

"Well then, let's try *your* word for it—*disappointed.* Do you know how sick and tired I am of disappointing you? I don't think I can do anything right. I might as well admit it. I'm stupid; I'm dumb; I can't remember anything!" I shouted.

"Why are you saying that?"

"Because it's true! Right? I mean, it's what you really think, isn't it? If you must know, Mrs. Disappointment, I got turned down for that stupid promotion that came up again at work! Yep, I am stupid and dumb." I felt betrayed by the tears rolling down my face.

"Honey, why didn't you say something?"

"Right. In front of Mr. I-just-made-my-first-million Jones? Don't even say that, Beth. You're the first one to get your hopes up and then be disappointed in me. I am not Superman! I get sick and tired of never living up to your expectations. You are always," I mocked her, "so 'disappointed' in me."

"That's not what I meant and you know it."

I could hear her voice, but it could not reach me. My heart was racing. I was headed toward a dark place. "You're just like my father!" I shouted from my cave. "You're acting just like my father when I lost that key. That stupid key." The room was spinning. I plunged into darkness. I was alone and scared. I felt hot tears stinging my eyes. I knew he was there. And then I heard his voice.

"Where's my key?"

"I don't know where it is." *Don't look at him; keep your head down.*

"You lost my key?"

I nodded shamefully. "It must have fallen out of my pocket." Tears spilled onto the rubber of my tennis shoes.

"You stupid kid!"

"I'll find it, Dad." *Anything to make the voice stop.*

"Darn right, you'll find it. You'll stay out there all night until you find it. Where was the last place you had it?"

Think, think. "I can't remember."

"You have a brain; use it!"

"I'm trying. It could have been the B building.

Yeah, I came out of the B building and, um, I saw a little kitten. . . ."

"Don't tell me you stopped to pet a cat?" he roared.

"It was only for a minute," I choked.

He exploded. "What did I do to end up with a kid as *stupid* as you? You can't remember anything! Now get out there and keep looking for my key."

I realized it had grown dark, and darkness was the only thing I was more afraid of than my dad. "But, Dad, I've already been looking for an hour."

"Did you find my key, son?"

"No, sir."

"Then get out there and keep looking."

"But, Dad, it's cold out, and it's getting dark. I mean, I could look better if I went home and got my jacket and a light."

"What did I tell you to do, son? No wonder you do bad in school. You can't even follow a simple instruction!"

"Let me just get a light and then I'll find your key."

"Aw, just go on home. Go home and get out of my sight. I don't even want to look at you anymore."

I just stood there. I didn't want to go out in

the dark, but I didn't want to go home either. *Let me disappear.* I stood there, filled with shame, unable to move.

"Go home!" he shouted, and pointed the way for a dumb kid like me. "Are you deaf, too?"

I wet my pants on the way home.

"Bill?" I could hear Beth. I wanted desperately to reach her, but the blackness would not let me go. She seemed like a light at the end of a tunnel, beckoning me, and I tried to move toward her, but *he* stood in my way.

"What were you thinking out there?" he shouted at me. More darkness, but I could make out the bleacher lights of my high school baseball field. "Or aren't you going to answer me?"

"I don't know," I mumbled. This time I was staring down at a pair of size-ten cleats, and I was determined there would be no tears on them.

"Darn right you don't know! What idiot would think to bunt in the last inning with two outs?"

"I thought I'd catch them by surprise."

"Well, you did that, all right. Son, did your coach tell you to bunt?"

"No, sir." I thought about lying.

"Do you realize you got your own man out and lost the game for your team?"

"Yes, sir."

"What do you think your teammates think of you, son?"

"Not much, sir." This was a routine to me by now.

"They're over there wondering what they did to end up with the stupidest kid in the world on their team!"

"I'm sorry, Dad."

"You are sorry, son," he said, and turned to walk away.

No more, I thought to myself. *Why do I go through this every game?* "Dad?" I choked.

He turned around. "What?"

"I . . . um . . . don't think I want to play baseball anymore."

"I see. So it's not enough that you're a loser, and you humiliate me and your teammates on the ballfield, but now you're just gonna walk away and quit?" He was incredulous. "You're never gonna make it in life, son. I'm telling you now so you won't be surprised."

I just stood there. My friends were staring.

"Is that what you want? To be a loser all your life? Answer me!"

"No, sir."

"Then I don't want to hear anymore of this quitting garbage!" He stormed away.

I stood there while my tears made mud on my cleats.

My fists were clenched, my face was a mask of anguish, and Beth was staring at me. I had no words yet for what had just happened. I wanted to hide. I wanted to curl up in a corner and wail. *Is this mental illness? Or simply madness?* I had no idea how long I had been standing there. It felt like twenty years.

Beth finally broke through the wall of silence. "Honey, I'm sorry about the job, and I'm sorry if I made you angry."

She had no idea what had happened to me. "It's nothing. I'm sorry I was late, okay? I let time get away at the office, and then I drove around for a little while." It felt like the argument was over, but what was going on within me was bigger than any argument we had ever had. Best just to let it go and get a good night's sleep. All of a sudden I felt very tired.

"What's going on, Bill? I feel like you're so far away." Maybe she did know what was happening to me, though I couldn't look into her eyes for support. I was still in a cloud of shame even though the storm had passed. I could sense her reaching for me. "Please tell me what you're feeling."

Was it safe? I deeply wanted to trust her and unburden my soul; I just wasn't sure how. I stole a glance toward her face. All traces of anger were gone. Her eyes were soft. She turned up one corner of her mouth in a warm half-smile. It really *was* her. It was okay. The words flowed quickly, as did the tears.

"I couldn't ever do it, Beth. In school, sports, work, I was always a 'stupid kid' who couldn't remember anything. I never found my dad's key, and he never let me forget it." I buried my head in my hands.

"Honey, that was a long time ago."

"I know, but I still feel so stupid . . . just like I did then."

The light dawned on Beth's face as she whispered, "I have said those words to you before. I said them tonight. I'm so sorry. I love you. I am not your father. There is no key between us." She wiped a stray tear.

"It's not just you, Beth. It's everything—work, the club. I can't get away from his voice. I guess I never did enough for my dad to love me."

"Would he have loved you—really loved you —if you'd found his dumb key?"

"Yes," I answered quickly, certain that if things

had gone differently on the night I lost his key, maybe my childhood would have been different. Something in my soul rose to the surface to convince me that it was not true. There were years of memories to support the fact that things would *not* have been any different. Yet, I still held onto false hope that I would one day be good enough for him. And today I knew I never would be. Overwhelming despair cried out from my soul, the soul of a little boy who longed to be loved by his daddy.

When the floodgate opened, thirty-four years of raw longing poured out—grief, anger, bitterness. I'd never felt so in touch with my own soul. All I could do was weep. I must have sat there for almost an hour. Beth sat with me, holding me at times.

Finally, bleary-eyed and nose-blown, I looked at her. "I've spent the better part of thirty-four years looking for my dad's key. And even if I'd found it, it wouldn't have made any difference."

"You are worth so much to me," she said. "Not for what you do. Thanks for what you do —I'm grateful—but please know that those things don't determine my love for you."

I nodded. I don't think I would have understood that statement had she made it just one hour earlier.

She continued, "It's like a relationship with God. . . ."

"Oh, don't bring God into this." Beth is forever trying to get me to go to church.

"No, Bill, wait. Maybe you can't see God or his love for you because of the way your father treated you. Why would you want to have another father when you couldn't get the love you wanted from the one you had?"

She was right. Another light came on. I felt as though I was waking from a long sleep.

"Unlike your dad, this Father offers you the unconditional love you've been searching for. His love isn't based on how many keys you find or on how well you perform."

She paused, and I stood there, absorbing the words she had just spoken.

"But your earthly father needs something from you," she said lightly.

"What?"

"Your forgiveness."

"For what?" I asked, incredulous.

"For the way he made you feel about yourself. And about God."

I didn't respond, and she didn't say anything else. But she had gotten through. My soul had opened enough for me to see how I ached to be loved with an unconditional love. And realizing that that ache would never be satisfied by my dad, I had taken the lid off an empty well that was now crying out to be filled.

Beth hugged me deeply and proceeded to finish the dishes. I sat in the kitchen until she was done.

2

A Mother's Journal

Tuesday, March 14

Motherhood is hard. I wish someone had told me that ahead of time. I mean, *really* told me that. Like sat me down, looked me squarely in the eyes, and said, "You might not survive this!" Don't get me wrong. I'm not knocking it, but I *would* like the freedom to say it is really hard, and sometimes it borders on the impossible.

Tonight we had dinner with Tom and Becky. I was putting the finishing touches on the meal with both kids wrapped around my legs while trying to tell Becky how overwhelmed I felt. At dinner she told four hundred stories of saintly mothers who never felt the way I was feeling. "It's all going to be worth it," Pollyanna assured me. I don't deny it. Heaven's worth it, too, but I'm not there yet. I hope I can just get a good night's sleep tonight!

Sunday, April 18

Why do my husband and children get tired of waiting for me after church? My husband says, "You never stop talking," but it's only because I spend so little time in the company of other adults that, once I get out, I don't want to go back. He also says, "You don't have anything to talk about." And I say, "I don't care. At least the conversation is in English." I spend my day in the company of foreigners, little people who don't speak the language yet. They cry, but they can't tell me what's wrong. It's enough to drive me crazy. So if I can have a shallow conversation on Sunday morning, it means a lot to me.

Who can I talk to about the way I feel? The pastor preached last week about being an overcomer. How can I be an overcomer when I can't keep my kid's shoes on? I glanced over at the pastor's wife to see if she felt like an overcomer, and she was nodding at what he was saying. I guess she is an overcomer; both of her kids' shoes were still on. I was nodding during his message, too—nodding *off*. Then my husband elbowed me. I hate that. He didn't get up four times in the middle of the night to clean up hunky pieces of . . . I'll spare the details. Just when I crawled back into bed, the alarm went off. My husband rolled over all groggy-like and asked, "Will you put the coffee on?" His *head*, maybe. . . .

Friday, May 5

Today was a really dark day. My husband walked in the door and said, "Look at this place! What have you been doing all day?" I said, "I've been tearing everything up, honey, and I'm just about done. I'm so glad I got finished before you came home. I'd hate to miss you being mad at me." Needless to say, the dark day didn't get any lighter when little Timmy ran to his daddy and said, "I'm glad you're home, 'cause Mommy's been yelling at me. Let's pray for her."

Thursday, May 25

I get so concerned that others might think I'm a bad mother, that I become a bad mother. I get caught up in that "Who's Who" among mothers thing. Does every mother face this, or is it just me? I try not to acknowledge it, but I know it's there, and sometimes, it eats my lunch. It's hard enough to face the fact that I will never have fame or fortune, but to be confronted daily by the fact that I can't afford to put my kids through private school or drive a new minivan is enough to send me right over the edge. I mean it. Sometimes my life is so shallow that that's all I care about.

Sunday, June 16

It's five-thirty in the morning, and I am desperately tired. It used to take me forty minutes to get ready for church. Now it takes me an *hour* and forty minutes. It takes him eighteen minutes and thirty seconds, and then he sits down with the comic strips and laughs his head off. After that, he comes into the bathroom where I am, just to ask, "Aren't you ready yet?"

I don't think he realizes that this morning I'll be packing diapers, wipes, baby toys, and Bibles for two kids, myself, him, and enough Squash Supreme for the whole church. Here's how it will go: We'll haul all the stuff to the car, survive the fight on the way there, haul it all inside to five hundred different places. I'll burn myself on the casserole on the way to the Fellowship Hall. He'll drop off one child at Sunday school, while I'll go on to the nursery to have the baby, kicking and screaming, surgically removed from my arms. I'll plop down in the sanctuary—I know why they call it that—only to realize I've forgotten my Bible, which was probably on the top of the car and now scattered in forty lawns along the way. By that time, I don't want a sermon. I want a *medal!* I won the thousand-meter church run!

Monday, June 17

I can't believe I'm sitting down to write, two days in a row. Timmy's at Caroline's, and the baby is sleeping. *Was* sleeping. . . .

Sunday, July 12

I used to like the children's sermon, until Timmy started going down to the front. Now my palms start to get sweaty during the hymn that precedes it. I start praying that the pastor will get healed from asking any questions. All those people that whisper while they're down there—you know, the ones that say, "Aren't they cute?" or "Look at that one!"—none of them have kids, or at least no kids that are down front. No, we parents are sitting on the edge of our pews, with clenched teeth, silently begging, *Please don't ask them anything.*

Today, the pastor asked the children, "Who has the greatest impact on our lives? Whose teaching and principles do we read and study and live by?" And my husband's son says, "Rush Limbaugh?"

Monday, July 28

Why am I so concerned about how other people see me? I thought I was concerned about my reputation before I had kids, but it's worse now. It's like my kids are a direct reflection of *me*. I find myself wishing that they wouldn't always tell the truth. Isn't that awful?

Monday, August 4

It is so hot. It seems like I want most the things I know I can't have: clean things, quiet time, white walls, cool air, and diapers with only pee-pee in them. Sometimes I wish *I* had a pacifier. I cried in Timmy's Cheerios this morning.

September 1

I am so lonely. I watched a soap opera today. I got so desperate for adult communication that I thought TV would be better than nothing. I was wrong. Loneliness is better than loneliness and depression. The women on those shows look like they had their babies out of their armpits!

I hate the way I look. The TV puts me at war with my own body. How can I make peace with my self-image when I'm tied, chained, welded to the way I look? There must be some value for who I am. So how do I move toward really liking myself? I know that looking in the mirror, saying, "I like me; I like me," won't help because I've tried it. I just hate myself for lying. It seems easier to pretend I'm okay and spend a lot of time avoiding the people who look like they have it all together.

Wednesday, October 25

God, will you meet me in all this despair? I tried to talk to Becky again about my feelings. She brought her kids over and we were making cupcakes. I confessed that I was struggling with my self-worth. I even told her that I felt so bad about the way I look that our sex life was really suffering. She looked at me like "Where's the door? I've got to get my children out of your house!" I thought it couldn't get worse until she sighed, and said, "Oh, I know just how you feel. I mean, I've never hated myself, but I got a really bad haircut last time."

I remember a Scripture verse from last Sunday. (*That* is a miracle in itself.) It said, "God will wipe away all tears." I always thought that meant that God would wipe them out—totally—and I would never cry again. Maybe it simply means that God will keep wiping them away. That I will feel his hand on my face, brushing away my tears. After my husband's gone to work, and the baby is napping peacefully after smashing four gazillion Cheerios in the carpet, and the *Victoria's Secret* catalog stares at me from the trash can, maybe his presence will be my comfort, and I won't have to reach for the remote or the telephone.

Friday, November 1

Tomorrow's my birthday. My husband asked me this morning in a real sexy tone if I wanted him to do something special for me. I said, "Yes," in a real sexy tone, "would you unload the dishwasher?"

Tuesday, December 17

Motherhood is hard, but it's worth it.

3

Another Fine Sunday Morning

If the kids and I had waited much longer, we could have gotten carbon monoxide poisoning in this garage," he said as I fastened my seat belt.

"It wasn't *that* long, and the garage door is up," I reminded him. "Besides, *I* had to get the baby's diapers."

He sighed meaningfully. "I already got the baby's diapers."

"Well, now we'll have extras."

We go through this almost every Sunday. My husband takes the children after I have gotten them ready, puts them in the car, and waits for me. Sometimes he just waits; sometimes he blows the horn; and on really bad days, he comes back into the house to get me.

"If you could be ready on time just one Sunday morning," he said, backing out of the drive with a squeal of the tires.

"If you hadn't steamed up the bathroom so bad," I shot back, "I wouldn't have had to do my hair twice, and I could have been ready earlier."

He looked puzzled. "Why didn't you just use the blow-dryer?"

"I forgot to tell you that it blew up yesterday. Jimmy tried to blow-dry the cat."

A shadow crossed my husband's face. "Is he all right?"

Sometimes I have a mean streak. "He's a little bald in spots."

"I meant Jimmy."

"He's fine. But I do think it scared him a little." My husband peeked in the rearview mirror to get a closer look at our number-one son. "You all right, Jimmy? No more appliances on the cat, okay?" He glanced at the clock on the dash to check the status of his race to church. He has a contest with himself every Sunday. The man has it down to a science. He looked troubled. He must be losing. "Well, if you'd gotten up thirty minutes earlier," he muttered.

"Not this again." I sighed. "If I could have had fifteen minutes worth of help from you . . ."

"You know I always have my Bible study on Sunday morning."

"Oh, don't I know it, honey! If the house was burning down and me with it, you'd still be having your Bible study." I was on a roll. "No way could you have that Bible study on Saturday night, when the kids are sleeping and everything is sort of peaceful. No! You've got to have it on Sunday morning, when I'm fighting for my life between the Cheerios-toss and the Where-are-your-shoes? contest!"

"Well, you'd better just take that up with God." He hit the car's blinker self-righteously for emphasis.

"Fine."

"Fine."

I've already mentioned, I have a mean streak. I started *praying* out loud. "Dear God, I pray for my husband. I pray that you'll deliver him from his self-centered, egotistical Bible study on Sunday morning. Lay upon his heart the need to help his devoted wife with the children and whatever else she needs him to do."

"Now, don't you go talking to God behind my back!"

"Oh, I wouldn't do a thing like that. You heard every word!" Smug as a bug in a rug.

"Fine. Two can play this game."

I looked nonchalantly out the window. I was hoping he was losing his race.

"Dear God," he began in his loudest I'm-praying-in-church voice, "I pray for my wife." I tried to notice the color of the leaves on the trees outside my car window. "I pray you'll help her understand my needs and be *submissive,* as the Word says she should be."

"How dare you!"

He continued praying, louder and more obnoxiously than ever. "God, help her know that my home is my castle. . . ."

He had crossed the line. "God, I pray you'd just zap my husband. He's nothing but a lazy couch potato. . . ."

". . . and whatever I say goes! No ifs, ands, or buts. . . ."

". . . and when it comes to helping me around the house, will he ever lift a finger? Nooo! When it comes to . . ."

"I mean when I come home from a long day at work, I don't need to hear nag, nag, nag. . . ."

". . . changing a diaper? Nooo! When it comes to . . ."

". . . All I want is a Coke and a smile, Lord! Is that too much to ask?"

". . . putting a dish in the dishwasher? Nooo!" We were both shouting at the top of our lungs. The baby had started to cry, and Jimmy was yelling in imitation of his parents.

That got my husband's attention. "Now you just hold on; hold on; *hold on!*" he shouted. "The Holy Spirit's trying to say something to you, and you can't hear him if you're praying!"

"What if the Holy Spirit wanted to say something to *you?*" I was seething.

"He already did, and it was about *you.* It says right here what I read in the Word this morning, 'Wives, submit to your husbands. . . .'"

"Look out!" I glanced up just in time to see us veer across the yellow line into the path of an oncoming truck. I grabbed the wheel and jerked the car back into our lane.

"I got it! I got it!" he yelled, pushing my hand off the wheel.

"You see there, if I'd been submitting, we would have had a wreck!"

"If you'd been submitting, I wouldn't have had to get my Bible out in the first place!"

"Oh, just park the car and be quiet. We're here."

My husband started talking into the rearview mirror. "Jimmy, you get your sister to Sunday school and turn in that offering this week." He glared at me. "We'll finish this in worship. Maybe God will say something to you by then."

"I doubt it." I glared back.

I unstrapped the baby and followed my husband out of the car. Jekyll and Hyde had nothing on us. The older kids rushed ahead, and my husband started across the parking lot. He was holding his Bible and grinning from ear to ear. "Hey, Bob Johnson, wait up."

About that time Delores Pickrell reached my side, looking as shell-shocked as I. "Hi, Delores!" We both smiled our biggest, phoniest smiles. "Another fine Sunday morning!"

· 4 ·

The Honest Couple

We went to bed angry and I wasn't sure why. As I lay there unable to sleep, I analyzed our evening. Tom and I had gone to dinner with another couple, and although pleasant enough, the event was far from a success. I wondered where it had gone wrong. My mind drifted back to our conversation right before we left the house:

"What time do we have to leave?" I had asked.

"In about ten minutes," Tom had replied.

"Do I look okay?"

"Yes, you look fine. Are you ready?"

"Do you think this outfit makes me look fat?"

"No, I don't. Really, you look fine," he assured me.

"I don't want to look fine, I want to look *good.*"

"Fine, you look good. How much longer are you going to be?"

"How much longer do I have?"

Tom scowled impatiently at his watch. "Eight minutes."

I checked the mirror again. "I don't think this looks good."

"I think it's fine." He hesitated. "Do you need anything?"

"Just a new wardrobe."

"With a closet full of clothes, you can't find anything to wear?" he questioned in utter disbelief.

"I hate all my clothes."

"Then just put on something you hate the least and let's go."

"You're more worried about being late than whether or not I feel good about what I'm wearing," I accused.

"That's not true. I just think you look great in anything," Tom added absently, "so it doesn't really matter to me what you wear."

"Really?"

"Really." He kissed me on the cheek. "Now finish getting ready and let's go."

"Okay."

Just a normal conversation, I thought in retrospect. So why had our evening gone downhill from there? What had that situation really been about? Maybe what we had *said* wasn't what we had *meant.* Just to be sure, I replayed our conversation:

"What time do we have to leave?"

(I'm going to be late.)

"In about ten minutes."

(Actually, it's twenty, but if I tell her ten, she may make it in twenty.)

"Do I look okay?"

(I feel really fat.)

"Yes, you look fine. Are you ready?"

(We don't have time to have the "Am I Fat?" discussion.)

"Do you think this outfit makes me look fat?"

(Depending on the way he says no, it could mean it really does.)

"No, I don't. Really, you look fine."

(I guess it does, but please don't go through your whole closet.)

"I don't want to look fine, I want to look *good.*"

(I feel like a cow in this outfit.)

"Fine, you look good. How much longer are you going to be?"

(Why are we always late?)

"How much longer do I have?"

(I wonder if I have time to change clothes.)

"Eight minutes."

(Not enough time to change your clothes.)

"I don't think this looks good."

(I've got to change.)

"I think it's fine. Do you need anything?"

(I'm going to the living room to read the paper.)

"Just a new wardrobe."

(I'm going to cry.)

"With a closet full of clothes, you can't find anything to wear?"

(She's not getting anything new.)

"I hate all of my clothes."

(I hate you for not helping me.)

"Just put on something that you hate the least and let's go."

(I hate you for making us late.)

"You're more worried about being late than whether or not I feel good about what I'm wearing."

(Wow, that was good!)

"That's not true." *(That is true.)* "I just think

you look great in anything, so it doesn't really matter to me what you wear."

(I wonder if she'll buy that.)

"Really?"

(If he's telling the truth, that was nice.)

"Really." He kissed me on the cheek. "Now finish getting ready and let's go."

(Whew!)

"Okay."

(I know he thinks I'm fat.)

I was beginning to see what was wrong. We hadn't been honest with each other at all. Our words were saying one thing, but there was an undercurrent of insecurity that we didn't bother to communicate with each other. Of course, my notion was pure speculation, but it was giving me a clearer indication of why we might be upset with each other. I began to wonder if there was even more under the surface. As long as I was speculating, I decided to think it through one more time:

"What time do we have to leave?"

(I'm going to be late.)

(I'm going to feel like a failure if I'm late.)

"In about ten minutes."

(Actually, it's twenty, but if I tell her ten, she may make it in twenty.)

(My reputation is riding on our walking out of here on time.)

"Do I look okay?"

(I feel really fat.)

(Do you love me even if I'm fat?)

"Yes, you look fine. Are you ready?"

(We don't have time to have the "Am I Fat?" discussion.)

(I can't handle your insecurities. I might have to look at my own.)

"Do you think this outfit makes me look fat?"

(Depending on the way he says no, it could mean it really does.)

(Will he lie to me, or will he love me?)

"No, I don't. Really, you look fine."

(I guess it does, but please don't go through your whole closet.)

(I can't win, so I might as well save my own skin. If I really convince her that she looks good, she might never change.)

"I don't want to look fine, I want to look *good.*"

(I feel like a cow in this outfit.)

(Will he love me if I look like a cow?)

"Fine, you look good. How much longer are you going to be?"

(Why are we always late?)

(If we're late and I look bad, I might just tell her she's fat.)

"How much longer do I have?"

(I wonder if I have time to change clothes.)

(How can I fix these terrible feelings?)

"Eight minutes."

(Not enough time to change your clothes.)

(I don't have time to worry about your feeling bad, because I'm starting to feel bad myself.)

"I don't think this looks good."

(I've got to change.)

(I want to feel better about myself.)

"I think it's fine. Do you need anything?"

(I'm going to the living room to read the paper.)

(I've got to get away from these terrible feelings.)

"Just a new wardrobe."

(I'm going to cry.)

(I want you to pull me out of this mess.)

"With a closet full of clothes, you can't find anything to wear?"

(She's not getting anything new.)

(I can't pull you out of this.)

"I hate all my clothes."

(I hate you for not helping me.)

(I hate myself.)

"Just put on something that you hate least and let's go."

(I hate you for making us late.)

(I hate myself.)

"You're more worried about being late than whether or not I feel good about what I'm wearing."

(Wow, that was good!)

(I wish that weren't true.)

"That's not true."

(That is true.)

(Why is that true?)

"I just think you look great in anything, so it doesn't really matter to me what you wear."

(I wonder if she'll buy that.)

(I don't want to talk about this anymore.)

"Really?"

(If he's telling the truth, that was nice.)

(Why is he running away?)

"Really." He kissed me on the cheek. "Now finish getting ready and let's go."

(Whew!)

(She's letting me get away with this.)

"Okay."

(I know he thinks I'm fat.)

(He hates me.)

It was making my head spin. Was that really what happened to us tonight? Something in me felt certain that it was. I was angry and insecure tonight. He was aloof and cold. All because neither one of us was brave enough to risk intimacy.

How could we ever be that honest with each other?

I fell asleep as I started thinking through another conversation we had had at dinner. . . .

5

Dear Daddy

Dear Daddy,
     This is the hardest letter I've ever had to write.

It was Christmas Eve, and I was five. I broke a lamp because I was running in the house, and you gave me a spanking. You were really angry with me, and as you sent me to my room, you said these words, "Santa Claus only visits good little girls." I lay awake the whole night, wondering if there would be anything from Santa because I had not been good. Although Santa did come that year and every year after, I thought it was because he felt sorry for me. I certainly had no illusions that I was good.

Remember the year I played baseball for

Tommy's Mini Mart? You used to come and watch my games when you could get away. I was always so proud to have you there. I wanted to do my very best so you would be really proud of me. I remember when I got up to bat, I could hear you yell, "Come on, hit that ball!" And if I got a hit, I'd always look up there in the stands where you sat with Mr. Bonner, and I'd wave. You'd shout, "Pay attention to the game."

If by some miracle I made it back across home plate, we would stop to get a snow cone on the way home. But you know, Daddy, I remember that if I didn't get a hit or if I tripped on my way to first base like I did during that one game, we didn't stop to get any snow cones. You could never have known how long those rides home were. Once, I got up the courage to say, "I'm sorry, Dad, I'll try harder next time." I said it to your back, and you kept on walking. I guess you couldn't tell me that it was okay to fail.

Do you remember Chris? He was my boyfriend my junior year of high school. You know, the one who took me to the homecoming dance. I think you were gone, but I remember showing you the pictures. He was the one who didn't wear socks. He was really special to me. He was all I knew to want in a boyfriend. He would open the car door for me; he would buy me little things, and he told me that he would really love me—if I slept with him. That probably surprises you, Dad. Chris said that sleeping together would prove we really loved each other. I figured my body was a small price to pay for real, secure love, so I did what he wanted. But it didn't prove anything. In fact, it sort of felt like the baseball game, Dad. Except this time, I was swinging for Chris's love. And I was a loser again.

Anyway, the years passed, and I went my own way. I know it was hard for you and Mom to watch me make most of the choices I made. In fact, you are probably wondering what is coming from all of this. I haven't said anything here to try to make you feel bad. I just want to help you understand me.

Last year, someone told me about Jesus. They said, "Jesus loves everybody just for who they are." I said, "Yeah, right. Where have I heard that one before?" And before I knew it, this rage was pouring out of me. "Santa Claus will only love you if you're a good little girl, and your daddy will only love you as long as you hit home runs, and your boyfriend, he'll love you as long as you give him what he asks for!" I never imagined I was so angry with you or the way I grew up. Later that night, I whispered—actually more like shouted—to God—"So what about *you?* What happens when *you* decide that I'm not good enough? Do I have to say, 'I'm sorry. I'll try harder next time'? Or 'No problem. It just didn't work out because I'm not pretty enough'?"

Dad, I felt the presence of God in a way that I can't even explain. I physically felt these arms wrap around me. I've never experienced anything like it.

Which is why I'm writing this letter. I want a relationship with you. I long to have you wrap your arms around me like God has. I have never had the courage to ask you this before, and I might not even send this letter once I get it written. Dad, do you love me? I really need to know. I don't do everything right, and I can't be perfect. But can you accept me . . . the way I am?

I have tried to show you my heart in this letter. I have truly found the ultimate Daddy who cares for me, but in the midst of his embrace, my heart still longs for yours. Could you feel the same way, but just not know the words to tell me?

I love you for free,
Your daughter

PART TWO

RESISTING GRACE

Thought: Do you really want God to treat you fairly?

A reward is something that is given in return for good or evil. A gift is something voluntarily given to another without compensation.

We understand rewards. They make sense to us. They keep us motivated, and they motivate others. But we have a little tougher time understanding gifts. In fact, most of the things we call gifts are really rewards. Even Christmas gifts are little more than rewards to all the special people in our lives for being special.

Except God's Christmas gift. Jesus was the first real Gift anyone had ever seen. But lots of people got confused and thought he was a reward. In fact, some still do.

You cannot receive grace if you think it's a reward for something you have done.

6

Above Minimum Wage

He arose a couple of hours before dawn. Fall was definitely in the air; his joints were a little stiffer in the coolness of the morning. He stared out over the acreage that had developed into his passion—his vineyard, the garden of his delight. He raised other animals and grew crops on his land—cattle, sheep, bees, and various fruits and vegetables—but his vineyard was the treasure. It had grown well for many years, but this year the harvest would be so great, he would need help to bring it in. Anticipation overtook him, and he climbed into his trusty, time-worn, gray pickup and went to town to hire some workmen.

At 5:30 A.M. he drove straight to the spot

where the unemployed laborers hung out. "I'd like to hire you all," the landowner shouted, rolling down his window.

"And we'd like nothing better," said Henry, the self-appointed leader of twelve. He was a thin man, not skinny, but strong. A hard worker who always met the demands of his boss-of-the-day, Henry walked toward the landowner, prepared to haggle. But there was to be no haggling today. The landowner was promising to pay above minimum wage for a full day's work and that was good enough. Henry and the others climbed into the back of the truck, excited about their prospective pay, and rode to the vineyard.

"So we'll all make minimum wage?" inquired one of the fellows in the group.

"He said *above* minimum wage," replied Henry.

"How much above?" asked Billy, whose mama was sick.

"Don't know. He didn't say." If everything went well, they could be looking at almost fifty dollars. Henry smiled. It was going to be a good day, after all.

Soon they arrived at the vineyard, and the landowner gave them instructions. He showed them how to harvest the grapes without damaging the vine or the fruit. Around eight-thirty, the landowner left the men to their work and headed back to town. About a half a mile before the main stoplight, he recognized "Moose," the town strong man. He honked his horn, stopped the truck, and waved Moose over.

"Done," said Moose, shaking the landowner's hand. "You just hired yourself nine good men." The landowner drove through town, picking up Moose's friends.

The men cackled with delight. "We're gonna make *above* minimum wage?"

Moose scratched his head. "That's what he said, fellas. And I shore wasn't gonna argue with him," he added. Moose figured they would make about thirty-six dollars, if they were lucky. And he felt lucky.

They arrived at the vineyard, and the landowner instructed them in their work. It wasn't long before he was heading off to town again.

This time, he pulled up in front of the Bristow brothers' place. All eight of them were in the front yard having a tobacco-spitting contest. Five of the more serious contenders were staring at the sixth who was squatting on the ground, spitting a long string of juice. The landowner got out of his truck and, watching where he stepped, walked over to them and gave them an offer.

"We'll need at least minimum wage."

"I'll pay you *above* minimum wage."

Buddy Bristow shook the landowner's hand. "Done. You just hired yourself eight good men."

As the brothers climbed into the back of the truck, Buddy called out to Sonny, the youngest, who was able to perform mathematical calculations. "What's it gonna be, Sonny?"

"Six hours at four bucks an hour? Close to twenty-five dollars, I'd say."

"He did say it would be *above* minimum wage," Buddy reminded him.

"Then it would be a little *over* twenty-five dollars." Sonny was smarter than Buddy and he liked to get the best of him.

Back at the vineyard, Henry saw the truck pull up again to let more workers out. "What's that crazy landowner doing?" he muttered to himself as he walked toward the Bristow brothers. Henry already had six hours of hard work under his belt, and he didn't want anyone cutting in on his pay.

Henry walked up to Buddy, who was already hard at work. "Howdy."

"Howdy." Buddy didn't look up.

Henry propped his chin on his rake as he looked at the horizon. "You fellas working 'til sundown?"

"That's what we've been told."

"How much you making?" Henry asked greedily.

Buddy spat a stream of tobacco juice mighty near Henry's foot. "Probably about twenty-five dollars."

"Sounds fair," Henry had to admit, and walked off.

Around three o'clock, the landowner headed back to town. It was pretty late to be hiring anyone; still, he had to try. Once in town, he made the first left and headed toward a hunch. Off Church Street, behind the warehouse, he would find more workers if today was the right day. And it was.

The landowner approached with caution. "I need some help," he said to Lefty, the unspoken leader of the men sitting on the ground playing cards.

"What kind of help?" Lefty never took his eyes off his cards.

"I've hired nearly thirty men today to work in my vineyard, and I need more help."

Jimmy looked at Lefty and laid down his hand, "Two pairs, ace high." No one was listening to the landowner; they wanted to see if Lefty would shoot Jimmy.

"I'm willing to pay you well," the landowner insisted.

In a flash, the card game was moved from behind the warehouse to the back of the truck.

"Hey, Lefty," Henry called, the minute the landowner was gone, "Your men are arriving here pretty late. Getting paid?"

"Yep." Lefty was a man of few words.

"Probably make about ten bucks, huh?"

"If that's what it is, then it's ten bucks more than I got now."

Meanwhile, the landowner set out one last time. When he arrived in town, there was no one looking for work. If three o'clock was a ridiculous hour to be hiring, then five o'clock was absurd. He had no more places to look, not even any more hunches to follow. He decided to head back to the vineyard, and he was preparing to turn right when a man with a white-tipped cane crossed the street in front of him.

The landowner shouted out his window, "Hey, buddy, can you come and work for me? I need some work done in my vineyard for one hour, and I'm willing to pay you what is right."

"Sure. I can help you a lot," the man said sarcastically. "Can't you see I'm blind?"

"Wonderful!" shouted the landowner, jumping out of his truck. He grabbed the man, helped him into the cab, and raced for the vineyard.

Sundown was approaching, and it would all be over soon enough.

The blind man's arrival went unnoticed by most. Henry shook his head at the foolishness of a landowner who would waste his time to hire one man—a blind one, at that—this late in the day to do the work he could have done himself. *Charity case,* he thought, and then turned his attention to finishing the work before him.

At sundown, the men clustered in groups, and stood speculating on their wages.

"Call the men and pay them their day's wage, beginning with the last man hired," the landowner said to the foreman.

The foreman handed the blind man his pay. The man was blind, not foolish. He knew there was *a lot* of money in his hand. Way more than he earned. Seeing his puzzled look, the landowner was at his side, "It's seventy-two dollars. Take it, my friend. Take it, and thank you."

The blind man made his way past all the others. He could not see them staring, of course. Nobody spoke for a full minute, and then Henry's twelve started jumping up and down, giving each other high fives. "Seventy-two bucks an hour! Oh, man!"

The foreman walked over to the men who had started up another card game and paid each of them seventy-two dollars. They had not seen that much money in their hands in . . . well, maybe *ever*. Lefty looked at the landowner and thanked him profusely, all the while shaking his hand vigorously.

The foreman had moved on to the Bristow brothers. They were not going to make twenty-five dollars, after all. They were going to make seventy-two dollars! "My wife's not gonna believe this," Buddy yelled, and then added, "if I tell her!"

It was party time at the vineyard. Lefty and his friends had thrown their cards in the air, and Buddy's brothers were dancing. Even the blind man came back to join the party. It was quite a sight. The landowner was overjoyed.

But for the rest, the drama of the moment had ended. Moose and the others who had been working since early morning knew that they were going to get seventy-two dollars, but suddenly, it didn't seem like so much. When the foreman called them to receive their pay, they did so without so much as a thank you.

Henry grew angrier and angrier. The gall of the landowner to pay as much to a blind man who had worked one hour as to the likes of them who had carried the burden of the work all day long. It was simply too much. The foreman called Henry and his men to receive their pay. "I'm not holding my hand out for that." Henry bypassed the foreman and went straight to the landowner. "That blind feller worked forty minutes and got the same measly money you're trying to offer us!"

"What did you agree to work for today?" the landowner asked Henry.

"*Above* minimum wage. But you paid that blind man . . ."

"Is seventy-two dollars still twenty-two dollars above minimum wage?"

"Yes, but you paid those greasy card players sixty-two dollars above minimum wage!"

"Take what I have paid you and go on. It is my money, and I'll spend it how I choose on whom I choose, because it is mine. Or are you envious because I'm good?" The landowner laid the money on the ground by Henry. "One last thing," he said. "Why do you have a problem with someone, other than yourself, getting something that they don't deserve?"

Henry stood in silent anger as the landowner returned to the party.

Then, leaving the money on the ground, he stalked off.

7

Don't Tell Anyone

Jesus did some really puzzling things. But I tell you what—some of the things that man *said* were a lot more puzzling than the things he *did*. Like the time he healed a leper. That was interesting in itself, but then Jesus told the leper not to tell anyone. Like all his friends were *not* going to notice. I've always wondered why he did that. Yesterday, I think I figured it out.

I run a small, southern, two-gas-pump convenience mart on the way out of town, just off old Route 40. I've been in business for nearly ten years, and I enjoy what I do. I get to meet a lot of folks, and my hours are pretty flexible, as long as I can get good help. Sometimes I'm not so lucky, and I have to pull a twelve- or fourteen-hour shift all by my lonesome. Yesterday was one of those days.

I had been in the store since 6:00 A.M. and had drunk way more coffee than I had sold, although we'd had a steady stream of customers throughout the morning. The temperature was already getting pretty warm, and it looked to be a scorcher by noon.

He came in to get an iced tea. I'd seen him before. He was an old man, and time had left its mark on his back. He couldn't stand up straight, but he was still the best fisherman this side of Barksdale County. I was happy to see him come back around.

I rang up the iced tea and we talked about the weather. He was headed up to a catfish farm that had just opened a couple miles west of here. The fishing would be too easy, he said, but he had a taste for catfish. He reached for his wallet to pay for the tea, but then stopped. He looked dazed. I wasn't sure what was wrong. Then he started rummaging through all his pockets, and his eyes darted back to the door he'd come in.

"Missing your wallet?" I asked.

"I don't know where it could be," he said, scratching his head. "I must've left it at home." He started to walk back toward the cooler to put back his iced tea.

"Hold on." I stopped him. "What change have you got in your pocket?"

He jingled what sounded like a few coins. Then he pulled out a fishing float, a nickel, a penny, and a big piece of lint, and laid them on the counter.

"I've only got six cents."

"That'll be fine," I said, collecting the money. I pushed the float and lint back toward him. When you own your own place, you can make these executive decisions. The old man looked confused. "It's okay," I reassured him. "Just take the tea and get on to your fishing."

He looked like he'd won the lottery. Okay, maybe just a bingo game, but he sure looked happy. "Iced tea for six cents." He laughed all the way out of the store.

It took me about two seconds to realize what I had done. I hopped around the counter, ran out the door, and shouted to the old man in his truck, "Don't you tell anybody I did that!" He drove off and I muttered aloud, "I'll have two dozen people in here demanding six-cent iced tea!"

He laughed and waved, but I was serious. And I was right.

It didn't take three hours for word to get from the catfish farm back here to me. Two old guys walked in, went straight to the cooler, and got themselves iced teas. They set them on the counter, cleared their throats a few times, and eyed me as if they were expecting something.

I rang up the purchases, and said, "That'll be a buck twenty-two." Well, one of them started hemming and hawing and acting like he couldn't find any money in his pockets. "Either pay or put the drinks back, fellas."

They looked hurt.

"You gave ol' Jeb an awfully good deal," one mumbled.

"I can do that; I own this place," I answered.

"Why won't you do the same for us?" the taller one sneered.

I leaned across the counter. "How much money you got with you?"

"None of your business!"

"Then just put the tea back and get out of here," I said, as I motioned for them to leave. They left under protest, said I wasn't being fair, and that I shouldn't be handing out six-cent iced tea if I didn't want everyone to get the same deal. I should have taken more care to make sure Jeb kept his mouth shut.

And this morning it hit me why Jesus told that leper not to tell anyone about his healing. Jesus didn't want people thinking they deserved the same deal the leper got. Those two fellas didn't want to tell me how much money they had in their pockets, but they wanted the same deal Jeb got. Anybody who thinks he has a right to something, probably doesn't. But the one who gives up his rights, like old Jeb, well, anything he gets is special to him.

But don't tell anyone I told you that.

8

The Purchase Plan of Heaven

The answer was, "The children."

The question was not, "Who is the biggest pain in the kingdom of God?"

The question was, "Who is *eligible*—able, most suited, accomplished enough—to enter the kingdom of God?"

Jesus, being the local expert and latest ambassador, said, "The children."

How odd. "I don't think I heard him right!" "Children are so undisciplined, irresponsible, unimportant."

How puzzling. "What have they done to deserve special treatment?" "They haven't been around long enough to build up their account."

"Children can't have any equity stored in the kingdom of God."

Then through the crowd, he came walking up to Jesus. Everyone grew silent, wanting to hear what this man had to say. He was dressed impeccably. He smelled of expensive cologne. He exuded importance. "What must *I* do to obtain eternal life?"

It was probably an honest question, but from his lips it sounded more like: "Is there one good thing I can do that will pay my ticket into the Magic Kingdom of heaven?"

or

"Hey, my credentials are impressive, but I don't want to leave any stone unturned, so give me the required list of good deeds that allows me to pass go and collect my eternal benefits."

or

"What is the bare-bones minimum level of obedience that will save my skin—if, that is, you really do have a kingdom?"

And Jesus replied, "It sounds like you are saying that stuff and deeds can be qualified as good, or that doing enough stuff or deeds can actually *make* one good. There is only one who is good, and that one is God, and God is good, not because of stuff or deeds, but simply because God *is* good. But since you are only interested in the purchase plan of heaven, all you must do is keep the commandments."

With an air of excited relief, the young man said, "I do that already. But let me be sure. Which commandments are you referring to exactly?"

And Jesus sighed, sad that this promising young man insisted that salvation could be bought. That eternal life was the reward for morality.

Jesus began naming commandments. Of the six that apply directly to the way we live with each other, he mentioned five: "Do not murder. Do not commit adultery. Do not steal. Do not give false witness. Honor your father and your mother."

The young man knew immediately that Jesus had left out one very important commandment. Had Jesus forgotten it? Or was this a loophole for people who had faithfully kept the other five? The man had been sweating it out, waiting for the last commandment to be mentioned as a requirement for heaven, but Jesus had not said a word about it: *Do not covet.* He was home free.

"All these things I have kept!" the young man said truthfully. "Now would there be anything else I lack?"

"Just one more thing," Jesus added. "If you

want to make your list of good works complete, go and sell your possessions and give to the poor. Then you will have real treasure."

The statement stung. The man stood there, exposed. Jesus had looked right through him. He did not have to reveal his sin. Jesus already knew what it was.

The young man did not hear anything else as he left, making his way through the crowd. In fact, he missed the best part—Jesus' last words to him: "Come, follow me."

Jesus called a lot of people to follow. But there was only a handful whose eyes he looked into as he issued the invitation, "Walk with me." But this young man walked away. With one exception, every man to whom he said that became a disciple.

Don't make the same mistake he made. He thought money could give him more security than God could.

There is no more foolish decision than insisting on paying your own way when the ticket has already been paid!

9

Brothers

I had been in practice for eight years. I had seen John Parker off and on for two. John originally came to me to deal with his workaholic tendencies. He was losing his marriage and he was frightened. We worked through much of his belief system and touched on some of his family issues. When we'd put enough of the pieces together to keep his life from falling apart, I saw John less and less. So I was quite surprised to see his name on my client list for the day, and I was even more surprised as his story began to unfold.

"It's good to see you, John."

He looked troubled and unsure about being in my office. He sat, fidgeting, and nervously looked around. "I didn't think I'd be coming back here again."

It is not uncommon for people to see a therapist during a particularly rocky time in their lives and then, as things run smoothly again, to assume that they will never need to go back. For some reason, there is a sense of personal failure when it doesn't work out that way.

"Why did you come today, John?" His face got cloudy, and his lip puffed as if he might burst into tears. At the moment, he looked about five years old. "Has something happened?"

"Yeah, you could say that." He was running the events in his mind like a movie. He fought for control. Clearing his throat, he asked me, "Do you remember my brother?"

I vaguely remembered a conversation we'd had about a year previously. He had mentioned his brother in passing, and I was remembering his comments as being less than positive. His brother had had a confrontation with their father. "The one who disappeared?" I asked.

"His name's Jimmy. He always liked to see just how far he could push things."

"What do you mean?"

"When we were little, he was always giving Mama and Daddy grief. He'd be the one to get hurt at school and then milk it for all it was worth. He'd lose stuff left and right, and when he was old enough to get money, well . . ." His voice trailed off as he fought for control. "Anything that could happen to somebody happened to Jimmy. Or he'd lie and say it happened.

"He also fought all the time. Back before Mama died, Jimmy almost got thrown out of school for fighting. Daddy went down to the school and fixed it for him. It would have killed Mama. Not one year after she passed away, he did get thrown out of school for good. Daddy couldn't stop it that time. Jimmy worked in town for a while and eventually moved out."

"I take it you were never close, even when you were younger."

"Never. I saw from the beginning what he did to our folks. Plus, he was always trying to get me to do stuff we weren't supposed to. I was forever saying, 'You're gonna get us both in trouble, Jimmy.' But he'd go on and do it and then beg for forgiveness."

I sat quietly as more pieces of the puzzle began to fall into place. As John talked about his brother, he exposed more roots of his workaholism. Dealing with people's issues is called a science, but it is more like trying to hit the piñata with a pole. I stepped up to swing.

"Let me see if I hear what you're saying. Jimmy got into trouble from the time you could remember. He wanted to involve you in a lot of his schemes, maybe even get you in trouble, too."

"Yes."

"What were some things that he wanted you to do?"

"When we were little? I don't see how that makes any difference."

"Indulge me."

He leaned forward in his chair as if he were going to tell me the secret code. "He would want to ride double on my bike, or something like that. Or he would stay at Robbie's house past supper time, on purpose. Worse, he would take money out of Daddy's wallet and try to talk me into going to the store."

"And you never did any of that?"

"Never."

"Then Jimmy would ask for forgiveness?"

"I'm telling you he had a lot of nerve."

"But *you* were a really good kid. You never had to ask for forgiveness for anything."

"You always do this to me. I came in here to talk about something that has me really stressed, and you're going off on some tangent."

"What are you so angry about?"

"I'm angry because you're sitting over in that

chair talking about my childhood, and I need to talk about today."

"What about it?"

"Jimmy came home three days ago."

Part of my job as a therapist is to avoid letting surprising things surprise me. So I kept quiet. I wanted to see where John would go with this.

"I just can't believe he came home," he said.

"Sometimes that makes sense after you've been gone."

"He's been gone for three years." He paused to let that sink in. "We haven't heard from him. No letters, no hi-the-weather's-fine postcards, no nothing. Is he dead? Is he alive? Day and night, that's all anybody talked about for a while, and then just as all the talk started to die down, here he comes home again. Just like that. Daddy and I were outside fixing the drainpipe. I was up on the roof and he was on the ladder. All of a sudden he lets out this big gasp. I'm thinking the old man's having a heart attack. Then he leaps off the ladder and starts running across the field. I look up in time to see him reach Jimmy. He starts hugging him and dancing around."

"How did that make you feel?"

"Oh, it didn't really bother me. I went in the house and got something to drink and left a note that I'd be back in a little while."

"I take it you didn't want to see him."

"You take it right."

"Have you seen him yet?" I asked.

"Yeah, I saw him later that night. I figured I'd go back to the house and maybe have a cup of coffee and find out what he'd been doing for the last three years. Except when I got to the house, I heard music playing and there were cars lined up on the street and the front door was wide open. The house was busting at the seams with people. I had no idea what was happening until I heard *him.* He was the same ol' Jimmy. Telling everybody a story in that loud tone of voice he always uses when he's had one too many. He finished his tale about the time I got to the open front door. I asked one of the neighbors, 'What's going on?' He turned to me with this big dumb grin on his face and said, 'Why, your little brother has come home!'

"I don't know. Maybe it was the smile, maybe it was the music or all the people, but I felt this rage well up inside me. Daddy threw *him* a party. I wanted to spit. My neighbor looked at me in the oddest sort of way and said, 'John? Aren't you going to come in?' I'd have rather had all my fingernails pulled out than step one foot in that front door. I turned and headed for my car.

"His voice stopped me. 'Son.' My dad was

coming across the driveway. 'Get away from me!'
I yelled. 'I've worked for you all my life. I didn't
take your money and run away. I didn't humiliate
you around town or get kicked out of school. I
didn't worry Mama half to death or steal money
when you weren't looking. I never did anything
wrong, but you never threw a party for me!' "

He was sobbing now. In our two years of ther-
apy, John had never shed so much as one tear.
His head was still in his hands. "I did everything
right. Why won't he love me? I never did any of
those bad things." He wiped his eyes and looked
at me. "Why did he throw Jimmy a party?" That
made him cry harder. "What else could I have
done for him? He never once gave me anything."

"Did you ever ask him for anything?"

He looked as though I'd touched him with a
cattle prod. "Why do I have to ask? Jimmy didn't
ask for *his* party! You sound just like *him.*" He
began to mock his father, " 'You know everything
I have is yours. You have always been here.' If he
knew how much I regretted staying, he would
never have said that. But no, he says, 'We must
celebrate, because your brother was lost to us and
now he is found.' "

"Why does that make you angry?" I asked.

"What's so great about being lost? He chose
to be lost. I chose *not* to be lost. You tell me

which is better. Why doesn't doing it right get any praise?"

I was listening to a man who, in his mind, had never done anything wrong. He could not see the lostness of his own soul. He wanted to hate his brother for "doing it all wrong"; instead, he hated himself for "doing it all right." He failed to see that in thinking that he had "done it right," he was wrong. And seeing his wrong would be the door to finding forgiveness and love. He had left no room in his soul for anyone but himself and his "rightness." And he was dying of loneliness.

I took another swing at the piñata. "How are you feeling right now?"

His voice was quiet and low. "Alone."

I leaned toward him. "Do you feel far away?" He nodded. "Like maybe you left home, too?"

I had insulted him. I could see it in his eyes. "I stayed. *He* left!"

"John, I know you stayed physically. But can you feel how far away your heart is? You might as well be wherever Jimmy's been for the last three years."

"How can you say that to me? I stayed! I'm not anything like him!"

I had to tell him the truth. "You *are* like him in your heart, John. You may never have done any of the things Jimmy has done on the outside, but you have done them all in your heart."

And that's all it took. The piñata burst and thirty-five years of pride, self-righteousness, and loneliness flowed out. "I hate you for being right," he sobbed in shame. "Just like I've hated Jimmy. Just like I hate everybody," he paused, "even myself." He wrestled with the truth of his own sin.

I leaned in close. I tried to look into his eyes, but he held them closed in shame. His sinful heart was exposed and aching. I whispered to him. "How would it feel to see your father leap off his ladder right now and run to you?"

It is for days like today that I am in practice.

PART THREE

KEEPING SCORE

The eighth definition of love in Webster's dictionary reads: "a score of zero, as in the game of tennis." But in tennis, or in life, the truth is crystal clear: Real love does not keep score.

Human love, on the other hand, keeps score constantly. It is always judging, evaluating, and grading. Sometimes it grades itself, and sometimes it grades others, but always it judges something. In fact, the characters in the next stories are such good scorekeepers, they are convinced that they are really loving each other.

But real love does not keep score.

We are never more like God than when we put down our score cards—and forgive.

10

Forgiveness? For What?

I was sitting on a park bench eating my sandwich when she told me I was going to hell. I usually come out here and eat lunch when the weather is nice. I only have thirty minutes, so I have to eat quickly.

She came walking up from nowhere—at least nowhere that I could see—and was in my face before I had time to swallow my last bite. She gave me this good news about my future and stared at me while I struggled to digest this revelation along with the end of my lunch.

"Now, I don't mean that in a bad way," she said, smiling really big.

"So I could go to hell in a good way?" I smiled

back. She looked confused, and I guessed she was new at this.

"Did you know that Jesus died to forgive you of your sins?" She glanced down at a big binder that she was clutching tightly. Then she stared at me.

"Thank him for me," I said, and reached for a cookie in my lunch bag.

"Thank him for me?" She opened the monstrous binder and started looking up something. I could hear her mumbling to herself as she flipped through pages.

"Okay, okay. Thank him for me? Where is that? Let's see . . . 'Inadequate, Indecent, Incessant! What to do with the Incessant Sandwich-Eater on a Park Bench.' "

She ruffled a few more pages, and I must confess I was absolutely terrified of what she would come up with next. I sat quietly munching on my cookie.

In a flash, she was on me. She grabbed my cookie and flung it into the air! "You don't need that cookie," she screamed, "You need Jesus!" Her face was about one centimeter from mine.

I gave my best I'm-not-from-around-here look and tried to speak with a little accent.

"Jesus? Who is dis Jesus?" It gets them every time.

She went scurrying back to her notebook and started mumbling, "Jesus, Jesus . . . Who is Jesus?" Then she realized she'd been had. "Whaddaya mean, who's Jesus?" She stared at me suspiciously. "Where have you lived all your life? Didn't you ever go to church?"

"No," I lied. She came charging back up to my face. *Wrong answer*, I thought to myself.

"Well, you are in trouble. You are so lucky I came along when I did. You need forgiveness, mister, and I'm here to tell you where to get it!"

This had gone just about far enough. "Forgiveness? For what?"

She was quick on the draw. "Moral filth, evil desires, wrongful living, debauchery, wild deeds, lust!" Then she said it again, although more calmly this time, "You're a sinner doomed to die and burn in hell."

"Now wait a minute, lady, you don't even know me. I am a great person. I mean, I don't drink; I don't cuss; I love my mom," the rhyme just came to me, "I never fuss." I was on a roll now. "I don't spit; I don't chew, nor run around with girls who do." She smiled a little, and I kept going. "I don't do drugs or own a gun. In fact, I never have any fun." I almost started laughing. "I don't drive fast," I lied, "and I don't fight. I am a good person, and I'm all right."

She looked at me, one brow arched. "Did you just make that up yourself?"

"Yep," I said proudly. It actually was one of the first truthful things I had said to her.

"That's cute." She giggled. Then she added, "Too bad you're gonna burn."

"Oh, good grief." I glanced in my lunch bag, hoping I had some food left. Perhaps if I ignored her, she'd go away.

"Get sanctified, or get french-fried," she said. I did my best to tune her out. "Get right or get left." She was getting louder. "Liberate or incinerate," she practically yelled. "Turn or burn!" she shouted, full force in my face. We were drawing a crowd. "Wake up, mister. You snooze, you lose."

"Stop it right now!" I snapped. "Sit down and be quiet."

She resorted to the notebook. "Who can say, 'I have kept my heart pure, and I am clean and without sin?' "

"I can," I answered flippantly.

She wasn't listening to me; she was preaching to the crowd. " 'For all have sinned and fallen short of the glory of God.' "

"Not me," I said in an aside to the bystanders.

" 'If you claim to be without sin, you deceive yourself and the truth is not in you.' "

"Yes, it is."

"No, it's not; no, it's not; no, it is not! Jesus said, 'You shall know the truth and the truth shall make you free.' "

"I *am* free."

"No, you love evil rather than good, falsehood rather than truth."

"I do not. Good grief, lady, get off this."

"I'm sorry, mister, but you have refused to believe the truth and so be saved. For this reason, God sends you a powerful delusion so that you will believe the lie, you who have delighted in evil rather than good, falsehood rather than speaking the truth!"

I sat there wondering how my lunch break had turned so weird all of a sudden.

Then she started to cry. "You're gonna spend eternity separated from God, our loving heavenly Father." Her words came out in little squeaks.

"Oh, come on, don't cry." I put my hand lightly on her shoulder. I was going to confess to her, but before I could say anything, she jerked her shoulder away.

"I'm not crying about you. I'm crying because the PBS system didn't work, and I'm going to fail my class if I don't convert someone."

"I see," I said slowly. It was making a lot of sense to me now. "What does PBS stand for?"

"Pearls Before Swine," she explained.

"I should have guessed." We sat there for a moment in silence. And the silence was wonderful. I debated about what to say next. "Can I see your notebook?"

"I guess so." She sniffled as she handed it over reluctantly.

The notebook weighed about a thousand pounds. "This is quite a lot of material," I commented casually while pretending to leaf through the pages.

"It's a full eighteen-month course, but I have been in the six-week kamikaze class."

"I see."

I turned in the notebook to page twenty-three, and read: " 'Whatever you must do, any tactics you must use to convince people that they are lost and doomed to hell are worth using. Stay in their faces, do not let up, and don't accept no for an answer. Their life in the kingdom is at stake.' " My stomach began to ache. I stared down at my own name and remembered the time in my life that I'd written this. My words looked up at me from the page, indicting me.

"Pretty good stuff, huh?" She was watching me read.

"Do you know this man?" I pointed to the author's name.

"Jim Bronson? The father of kamikaze evangelism?"

I nodded.

"I've only heard about him in class."

"Pleased to meet you." I held out my hand to shake hers. Her face was a cloud of confusion. "I'm Jim Bronson."

"But you're not even a Christian," she sputtered.

"Yes, I am." I laughed. She was not laughing. "I wrote this stuff about twenty years ago. I was into evangelism to make myself important to God. I've changed a lot since then." I paused. "What's your name?"

"Priscilla," she answered.

I leaned in closer and whispered, "Priscilla, why are you doing this?"

"Doing what?" she whispered back. "Sharing my faith?"

"No, sharing someone else's faith." I pointed to the notebook. I thought she might jump up and start preaching again, but she just sat solemnly. "Do you keep score?"

She seemed quite surprised that I knew the

term. She opened the binder to the inside cover. "I'm up to eight."

"And if you don't get to ten you're going to fail your class?"

She nodded sadly.

"Of those eight marks, do you remember any of their names?"

"Just my cousin Julie." She ducked her head a little sheepishly.

"I didn't know any of the people's names that the marks in my binder represented, either. Nor did I care."

Priscilla looked down. "I guess I just wanted you to accept Christ so I would look good to my class." She started to cry louder. "It's true." Then she started to blubber so loud all of the pigeons flew away. "I'm a head-hunter for God!" More wails.

"If I hadn't written that material, there might not be a class for you to impress," I admitted. "People might be sharing their faith because it meant something to them, rather than because they were going to win a prize from their church."

"You heard about the microwave?"

We both laughed. "Priscilla, I've got to get back to work. I'm sorry if I messed up your evangelism attack."

"It's okay. You really made me think, or maybe I should say, *re*think."

I stood to leave and she stuck out her hand. "I'm glad you're not going to hell."

"Me, too!" I chuckled.

11

The Unforgiving Cook

The disciples seemed to spend a lot of time just standing around talking. One day, during one of their conversations, Peter was sort of fidgety over in the corner. He had a question he really wanted to ask Jesus, but he wasn't quite sure how to phrase it.

"Um, Jesus? How many times do I have to forgive someone?" He paused to study Jesus' face. "I was thinking seven."

"I was thinking of a bigger number, Peter," Jesus answered kindly.

"Eight?" Peter had this one guy in mind from the pier who had been giving him a lot of trouble.

"A lot bigger."

"Twenty?" Peter asked in desperation. He couldn't go much higher.

"Forget the numbers for a minute, Peter," Jesus said. "In God's kingdom, forgiveness looks like this. . . .

There was a king who wanted to settle accounts with his servants. He opened the royal ledger and began to study who owed what. He looked over the accounts of the doorman, the butler, the parlor maid, the housekeeper, the kennelman, the seamstress—all the household help.

During this lengthy process, the cook was brought before him. The king turned in the ledger to the cook's page. His account continued on to the next column, and on to the next, and on to the next two hundred pages!

"Four bazillion dollars!" cried the cook. "How'd I do that?"

The cook had no means of paying it back. He added up his salary for the next fifty lifetimes— although as of yet no one has had more than one —and it still wasn't enough.

So the king ordered that the cook and all his possessions, his wife, his children, and even his dog, be put out on the auctioneer's block. They were going to be sold as slaves. The bidding began.

"Five dollars for his shirt!" called a man in the crowd.

"Not my shirt!" cried the cook.

"Six dollars for his shoes!" shouted another.

"Not my shoes!"

"Two bucks for the dog!"

"Wait a minute, he's worth more than that!" interrupted the cook. "I mean, not my dog." "Please!" he cried, and he fell down on his knees before the king. "Give me a chance and I will pay it all back—somehow!"

The crowd broke out in laughter. They looked at the king to see how hard he was laughing. But the king wasn't laughing.

"Give me a chance and I will pay it all back," the cook insisted.

"But it would take you fifty-five lifetimes!" shouted a man in the crowd.

"I'll find a way!"

All eyes were on the king, who actually seemed to be considering the cook's ridiculous offer. The crowd watched in complete amazement as the king brushed away a tear.

Then the king held up the royal ledger high in the air, and a cheer went up from the crowd. He slammed the ledger shut with the loudest bang that anyone had heard for a long time.

What did it mean? No one could ever remember the king closing the ledger before on an unpaid debt. Did it mean that the debt was paid, or did it mean that the cook had been granted his request for more time? There was a babble of voices as the matter was discussed among the crowd.

But the cook was ecstatic. "I got another chance. I don't have to pay him back yet!" It hadn't crossed his mind to wonder if the king had forgiven him. He was so happy to have been granted an extension, that he danced his way off the auction block and back to the castle to prepare a great lunch.

No sooner was he back in the castle than he ran into the parlor maid, who owed him ten dollars.

"Mildred!" he called out, grabbing her around the neck. "You owe me ten bucks! When are you going to pay me back?"

The parlor maid couldn't answer very well while she was being strangled, but she did manage to croak out, "Give me more time, and I'll pay you soon."

"I have a big debt hanging over my head, and I'm not letting you off the hook anymore!" He called the guards and had Mildred arrested and thrown into jail, until she could pay back what she owed him.

But castles have eyes and ears. The chamber maid, the kennel man, and the butler had been in the crowd when the king slammed the ledger on the cook's debt. They went straight to the king to tell him what had happened.

The king was furious and summoned the cook.

"Vichyssoise?" the cook offered.

"You wicked servant!" said the king. "Think of all the money I forgave you! And look at what little you refused to forgive!"

"Forgiven?" This was a brand-new word to the cook.

"I showed you mercy," continued the king, "and you showed her none! Now, I will show you none!"

The king had the cook thrown into the dungeon to be tortured until the debt could be repaid.

Then Jesus turned to Peter and said, "This is how my heavenly Father will act toward those whom he has forgiven who choose not to forgive others." And the matter never came up again.

12

Ledger People

Hi, honey. You're home early." Sally smiled as Ken walked into the kitchen. She gave him a peck on the cheek and returned to the head of lettuce she was washing at the sink.

"You know, it's the third time this week that I've been home early."

"I guess you expect me to write that down," Sally said, wiping her hands on her apron.

"Oh, just when you get a chance."

Sally pulled her red ledger from the front pocket of her apron and scribbled by Ken's name: *Home early, +1.* "How was work?"

"Not so good. You know that proposal I was working on? I submitted it to Mike and Robert today, and I overheard Robert say something to

Mike about it as I was leaving. It wasn't very positive. When I went to write it down in the ledger, I noticed that it was the third negative comment he'd made about my performance this week. He's coming up short here lately."

"I'm sorry, honey, but I know how you feel. My mother has three pages of minuses in my ledger, and I'm not sure how to tell her."

"I'll tell her," Ken teased.

"That's okay."

"What's for dinner? I'm starving."

"Lasagna," she said with pride.

"Okay, okay, I'll write it down." Ken opened his ledger and scribbled the entry by Sally's name. "Hey, look at this, that's twelve pluses in a row for you."

Sally was not as surprised as he was. "I've been trying," she said sweetly.

"That's quite a turnaround from last week."

"Honey, I said I was sorry." She was getting defensive.

"Yeah, but the *proof* is in the ledger. That was some shopping spree. The lasagna gets you out of the hole and pulls your balance back up."

"I made strawberry shortcake for dessert."

"Are you planning another purchase?"

"No."

"All right." Ken made another entry in the ledger. "One more point."

"Wait, I should get two for that."

"Why two?"

"One for the strawberries and one for the shortcake."

Ken recorded Sally's points and set his ledger down on the table. "What is this receipt here?"

"It's from a gift I bought for Susan."

"What occasion?"

"She bought me one," Sally said uncomfortably. "Yesterday she dropped by with this little container of soup mix in a jar with a bow."

Ken was incredulous. "So, out of the blue she just bought you a gift?"

"Yep."

"Were you one down?" He was slightly suspicious.

"Not by my records."

Ken whistled softly through his teeth.

"So I bought her a bath basket and dropped it by her office, so I could sleep tonight."

Ken laughed. "Is that why you were thrashing about last night? You kept me up long enough to subtract some of your points." Sally started to object, but Ken stopped her. "I'm only kidding. Where are the kids?"

"Jenny is at Elizabeth's." Ken started to look a

little concerned, but Sally caught it. "Elizabeth was here yesterday, so it's fine." Ken looked relieved. "And Billy is in his room."

"I thought Billy had football practice this afternoon."

"He did, but I didn't let him go. He forgot his social studies homework for the third day in a row. This is the third week that his balance has fallen below acceptable levels."

"So what is he doing in his room?"

"Well, he's trying to come up with a plan that will net him five pluses by tomorrow."

"Poor kid."

Sally was adamant. "Don't start that. He brought this on himself. He's old enough now to keep up with his own ledger." She smiled. "This afternoon he said, 'Mom, do you think I could just have a spanking instead?' "

Ken laughed out loud. "Can you believe some parents actually treat their children that way?"

"Oh, I forgot to tell you. Bob wanted you to call him when you got in. He wants to borrow the mower tonight."

"He kept it four days last time," Ken whined.

"Honey, you told him that was okay."

"Yeah, but I didn't really mean it."

"Ken, it's okay if it stays on the ledger a little while."

"Yeah, it's not like I borrowed first."

"Right. That's the worst."

Ken headed toward the living room. "What time is dinner?"

"In about thirty minutes."

"I'm going to read the paper."

"You don't get any points for reading the paper," Sally quipped.

"That's okay. Some things I do just because I enjoy them."

"You would get some points if you went running."

"But I don't enjoy that." Sally was always after him to exercise more. They had already had words this month from Sally taking points off because his jeans didn't fit anymore. He sighed. "Do I really need the points?"

"Yes." She reached for her ledger and scanned his pages. "Badly."

"Badly? How badly?" He couldn't be that far behind.

"Let me put it this way: Your point balance makes Billy's look great."

Ken was indignant. "No way! I was home early three times this week."

Sally flipped back a couple of pages in her ledger. "But you were home late four times last week."

"I was putting in overtime last week. That should not count as being late! Besides, I was only putting in overtime because you quit work!"

"Did you subtract points from me for quitting work? That was a mutually agreed-upon decision."

Ken glanced down at his ledger. "Just a few."

"You are so sneaky." Sally picked up her pen. "Minus ten!"

Ken shouted, "From what? I don't have any points left. You take away my points like it's a hobby!" He stared at Sally in horror as a tear trickled down her face. "Now don't you start crying!"

"Minus five more," Sally said through her tears.

"I did not make you cry! You started crying on your own. That's only two points."

"I can't stand you!" she shouted.

"Ooh! Minus ten big ones!" Ken scribbled furiously.

"Wait, I did not say 'hate,' I said 'can't stand.'"

"No, but you meant hate."

Sally was grasping at straws. "It doesn't matter what you mean; it only matters what you say."

"Oh, is that it?" Ken was trying out a new theory. "It doesn't matter what you mean; it only matters what you actually say, huh? Just take the heart right out of it, Sally." He looked smug. "Let's see now—compliments are one point each, aren't they? Honey, you look wonderful," he stated flatly. "Your hair just shines," he droned on.

"Stop it right now."

"Kisses are worth two points, aren't they, Sally?" Ken kissed her on the cheek. "Start writing it down, Sally. I'm already up to four points. I should be out of the hole by dinner."

"I'm not writing anything down."

"Why not? I'm getting all my points the old-fashioned way. I'm earning them."

"You don't mean what you're saying." Sally was sobbing now.

"It doesn't matter what I really mean, does it? It only matters what I say. Isn't that what you said? Or does the rule only apply to *you?*"

"You're not being fair," she spat.

"What does fair have to do with anything?" he demanded. "I spend my life working my way back to the black. That's fair? That's what love is about?"

"Love is about your doing as much for me as I am doing for you."

"And what if I don't want to?"

Sally felt as if she had been struck. "What?"

"What if I don't want to do this anymore? What if I'm sick and tired of pluses and minuses, points and ledgers? What if I wanted to do something for you, just because I loved you?"

She thought for a moment. "I'd give you some bonus points for that."

"Sally, stop it! Don't you see that's what I'm talking about? We live our lives ruled by this thing." He held the ledger in his hands, turning it over and over. He stared at his name engraved in gold. Sally had had it done last Christmas. He felt sick at his stomach. "I'm through," he said quietly. "I'm closing my ledger for good."

"You can't just close your ledger for good." She laughed a scared laugh.

"I just did." He was feeling better by the minute.

"What about all my points?" There was panic in her voice.

He said it slowly. "They don't matter to me anymore."

"Well, they matter to me, Ken. I've worked hard for those points."

"I know you have, and I love you." He hesitated. "Isn't that enough?"

It took her a long time to answer. "I don't know."

"I see. So you love your point balance more than you love me?"

"I didn't say that. It's just a whole lot easier for you to close the ledger because you're behind, because you're losing." Her tears came faster now.

He lifted her chin and looked into her eyes. "I *am* losing, Sally. I'm losing you, I'm losing Jenny and Billy, and I'm losing me."

"What about all your minuses?" There was hurt in her voice. "What are you going to do about those?"

"I could never turn them all into pluses."

"You could try."

"There aren't enough lifetimes." He swallowed hard. "I'll just have to ask your forgiveness."

"Just like that? What about next time, and the time after that?"

It dawned on him like the sun. "If the ledger's closed, where will you write it down?"

"If the ledger's closed, Ken, how will you do what you are supposed to do?"

"And what am I supposed to do? Keep score? Or love you?"

Her lips had trouble forming the words. "Love me."

"I don't think I can do that as long as we are keeping score. If I'm trying to win, I can't love you well."

Then the tiniest voice cried out the biggest fear of her heart, "But do you really want to love me?"

"I really do."

She was skeptical. "For no points?"

"For no points."

"No bonuses?"

"No bonuses." He slid the ledger out of her hands and put it on the table by his as he pulled her into his arms. A feeling of freedom washed over both of them. Suddenly Ken broke away. "I'll be right back."

"Where are you going?" Sally asked, concerned.

"I've got some good news for Billy."

13

The Kingdom of Thanks

I have created a kingdom. I am the king and the people to whom I give gifts are my subjects. I rule them through their gratitude to me.

I bought my wife a birthday present a month ago. The item—a rice steamer—was on back order, so I created a decorative postcard to announce her future-but-promised gift. I reigned supremely on that day, for this gift was at the top of her list as one of those great kitchen gadgets she had to have. (It is important in my Kingdom of Thanks to give just the right gift, or my power could be diminished by lack of appreciation. One year I gave her a vacuum cleaner for her birthday, and I had no power whatsoever.)

I soon forgot about the back-ordered rice

steamer, and a month went by. With much embarrassment my wife asked me about her gift. Sensing a small rebellion on the horizon, I called the store. The item was still on back order, so my wife suggested that we look for one somewhere else.

It did not take us long to find the steamer she wanted. She was genuinely glad to have it and told me so. She told me how much she loved me, and how special her birthday present was. I sat on my throne proudly. "Why don't we use it tonight?" I decreed. She readily agreed and we rode home together in my carriage, holding hands. I had kingly hopes for later that night. (Therein lies the payoff of ruling in the Kingdom of Thanks: I give generously so that I can get generously in return.)

We arrived home and began making plans for dinner. "What do we want to eat tonight that we can cook in the new steamer?" she asked me.

"Pancakes?" I joked.

She rolled her eyes. "What about rice and broccoli?"

"Sounds good to me." I was happy basking in my control.

"Okay, what else?" She was concentrating.

"Chicken."

"We can't cook that in the steamer."

"I know, but we can have it with the rice and broccoli," I suggested.

"One problem. Do we have any of these foods?"

"No," I said, staring into the bare cupboard.

"Nothing?"

"Well, we have a package of powdered teriyaki sauce."

"Okay, one of us needs to go to the store," she decided.

But I am the king. "Which one of us?"

"You can go."

"Why me?"

"I have to call my mother to check on her test results."

"What tests?"

"The tests they ran on her eyes."

"Did I know about this?"

"Yes, I told you last night."

"I don't remember."

"You never remember, but I did tell you."

I felt my power slipping. "Okay, okay—you told me. I forgot. Sorry."

"That's okay. You just need to go to the store. We need broccoli, chicken, milk for tomorrow morning—we're almost out—some liquid teriyaki sauce. . . ."

"What's wrong with the powdered stuff?" I asked.

"It's powdered, for one thing. And it's old. We've had it since your brother lived with us, two years ago."

"It's probably still good."

"Liquid teriyaki sauce," she insisted, "and pineapple juice to blend with it."

"Okay, broccoli, chicken, milk, teriyaki sauce —liquid—and pineapple juice. Five things. I got it. I'll see you in a few minutes."

"And don't forget the rice."

"Oh, yeah, rice." I made a mental note.

"You'd better write it down."

"I don't need to write it down. I can remember." I am the king, and kings don't forget things at the store. "It's only five items—broccoli, chicken, milk, teriyaki sauce, and pineapple juice."

"And rice. You'd better write it down."

"No, I don't need to write it down. I'll remember."

She gave me a skeptical glance. "Trust me."

"It's all right up here." I tapped my forehead. "See you in a few minutes. Tell your mother I prayed for her."

"But you didn't even remember."

"I'm praying for her now. Just tell her. It'll make her feel good."

"No, it will just make you look good."

"Fine, don't tell her. I'll be back."

"Oh, get me some razor blades, too. I'm out."

"Okay, razor blades."

"You'd better write it down."

"I got it."

"Don't forget."

"I won't."

And I was out the door. I hated going back out, but my wife was feeling great about me, and I did not want to ruin it. Besides, to add gratitude upon gratitude could only increase her indebtedness to me. I felt giddy with power.

Fortunately, the grocery store was not too far from the house, and I could take some back roads to avoid the traffic. Of course, the grocery store was packed with people, but I knew I needed fewer than ten items, and I had cash. So I quickly scooped up my items: broccoli, teriyaki sauce—*why don't they shelve that stuff with the other sauces?*—pineapple juice—*why does this only come in four-ounce cans?*—chicken—*I guess we want boneless/skinless. Whoa, it's so much more expensive, but that's okay; I'll splurge*—and milk—*I hate skim, but if I don't buy it, I'll get sighed at.* Oh, razor blades—*I hope this is the right kind—oh, well. Okay, that's everything. Is that every-*

thing? Yep, let me just get out of here. And don't forget to ask about my mother-in-law.

My wife was just hanging up the phone when I walked in the door.

"Did you have any trouble?" she asked.

"Nope," I replied, placing my one bag on the countertop. "It was crowded, but I managed. Even remembered your razor blades. I hope this is the right kind."

"It is. Perfect. Thank you," she said, as she started taking the food out of the bag.

"How's your mother?" I had remembered.

"Good. Her tests showed that her eye nerves were fine. Apparently her pain was caused by excessive strain."

"Oh. That's good news." I examined the steamer she had pulled out of the box and set up. She probably had managed to read the directions, too, while having an in-depth conversation with her mother. She amazed me sometimes. I picked up the steamer to investigate it. "Is this thing going to work?" Secretly, this was a gratitude check. I might even get a kiss.

"Yes." Pause. "Honey, where's the rice?" *No kiss.*

Uh-oh. "What rice?"

"You forgot the rice, didn't you?"

"Yeah, I guess I did."

"Why didn't you make a list of what you needed? I told you you'd forget. Why didn't you listen to me?"

"I did listen. I just forgot. I'll go back to the store and get it."

"No, you didn't listen. Or else you would have written it down."

"Just because I didn't agree with you doesn't mean I didn't listen," I countered.

"No, that's not it. You didn't want to talk with me. You only wanted to do what you wanted to do."

"Listen. I just forgot. It's no big deal. I'll go back out and get some rice." I felt my kingdom slipping away. "I'm the only one who's inconvenienced. Don't make such a big deal about it."

"It *is* a big deal." Her voice was taking on that admonishing tone I hated. "I don't want you to go back out. We have this problem over and over. You only listen to me when it's convenient."

"I do not!" I was beginning to get angry. The last thing I wanted was an argument. For goodness' sakes, I had just run to the store *for her,* so that she could talk to *her* mother, and after buying a food steamer—*for her.* What else did she want from me?

"You didn't want to make a list," she pointed out. "You didn't hear one word about my mother last night because you were watching some game, and you forgot about my birthday present until I reminded you."

"What are you talking about?!" I knew exactly what she was talking about.

She was right. I did not want to pull out pen and paper to make a list because I just wanted to get the trip to the grocery store over with. I did not hear her speak to me about her mother because I was watching a ball game and I wanted to be left alone. And I *did* forget about her birthday present because I had already gotten the praise for it a month before.

But she didn't know any of that. So why was she railing on me? I had just given her a present, for crying out loud. Where was her gratitude? Okay, maybe I did forget a few things, but she sure was being ungrateful. She was lucky she had married me and not some jerk who abused women. "You are really ungrateful," I told her.

She started crying and left the room. When she closed the bedroom door, I felt it in my soul. We had gone from a small rebellion in the Kingdom of Thanks to an all-out insurrection. I grabbed my keys and stalked out, being sure to slam the front door. I would get her rice, but I knew she would not be grateful. But instead of starting the car and going to the store, I sat in the driveway.

I really wanted to be angry with her. "Now what went wrong?" I shouted to myself. "How much do I have to buy for her? I did everything right!" But my words just bounced around inside the car like a BB in an empty tin can.

The Kingdom of Thanks is the loneliest place on earth. It is a dead existence. C. S. Lewis said, "I may act kindly, justly and correctly toward my wife and yet withhold the giving of myself, which is love." That's the way I want it to work in my kingdom. I do not want to give of myself, so I give gifts instead. Hoping that if she is grateful enough, I'll get what I want. But who wants to love a king who only wants power? She wants to connect with me, to talk with me about her mother, but I want to "play" connected, to get what I want in return. *O God, have mercy on my soul. I am so lonely.*

14

The Coach

She was sweating profusely. "Ninety-eight, ninety-nine, one hundred," she whispered, out of breath. "I just did one hundred deep knee bends." But her satisfaction was short-lived.

Do you think that makes you look like Cindy Crawford? Do you know how much she weighs?

"I'd hate to guess."

And she's five feet taller than you are!

Kathy accepted the inner rebuke and decided to do her push-ups. She had been working on strengthening her arms for weeks, and she could now do five push-ups in a row. She was finished with her warm-ups and was ready for her morning walk. She usually walked with her neighbor, but Janice was out of town today, so Kathy was on her own.

She was stretching her calf muscles by pushing against the garage door frame. Since the door was up, she stared inside, appalled at the accumulation of years.

If you were any kind of housekeeper, you'd put that stuff where it belongs.

"But it doesn't belong anywhere. Most of it is junk."

Then why haven't you sorted through it and given it to the homeless shelter?

"I'll think about it when I get back."

Kathy had a fairly peaceful walk. She usually walked about a mile. She had been trying hard to get in shape. Having put on a few extra pounds over the last few years, she desperately wanted to shed them. She was only a block from the house when the Coach spoke again.

You are so fat! How could you let yourself get this way?

Kathy tried to ignore the voice as best she could. She picked up the pace and finished her walk. Her husband was up when she went back into the house, and she pointed to the coffeepot that was waiting for him. "I'm gonna take a shower. Would you mind waking the girls?" He grunted, and she headed for their bathroom. She undressed, trying to resist the temptation to look in the mirror as she stepped under the surging hot water. If she didn't look any thinner, she knew it would only summon the Coach.

She made breakfast for the girls and got them on the bus. Jack left for the office shortly thereafter. Kathy had a ten o'clock appointment, so she had plenty of time for an extra cup of coffee.

You could have fixed more than toast for your family this morning.

"That's all they wanted," Kathy protested. Couldn't she just enjoy a cup of coffee in silence? "Besides, none of us needs to be eating a high-fat breakfast."

None of us? Or just you?

"Okay, just me. I'll do better tomorrow morning." Jack did look a little disappointed when she put dry whole wheat toast down in front of him. "I've just got to be a better wife and mother," she said sadly to herself.

Yes, you do!

Kathy figured she had just enough time to do her Bible reading before she had to go to work. She reached for her red New American Standard Bible and her devotional book.

Maybe you can "do" enough today for God to really love you.

"I'm off to a pretty good start. I mean, I've

exercised and showered, fed my family, and now I'm going to have a quiet time."

Well, that's pretty good, but what else have you done? Surely you don't think God's gonna be happy with your measly little quiet time?

"Maybe he will be. He's supposed to be a loving God, right?" Kathy was only half-joking. She prayed for wisdom and understanding, she read her Bible, she wrote down her insights, she thanked God for her children and her husband, and she even wrote a check to a missionary they knew overseas. She felt good. Her quiet time was a success, and the Coach was silent. Until lunch.

Kathy's ten o'clock appointment was a no-show. She worked part-time—cutting hair at a friend's studio—and sometimes that was the nature of the hair business. It did not make her feel any better, though. She ran a few errands and then stopped to get a salad at Wendy's.

You're still fat. You might as well just order what you usually do. Unless you want to be really great—then you'll get a side salad with no dressing. But the choice is yours.

"I was planning to get a salad already, thank you."

But you were planning to get dressing, thank you. If you really want to be thin and beautiful, you will forgo the dressing.

"I'll have a side salad with no dressing, please,

and a large water with lemon," Kathy said to the ninety-eight-pound girl behind the counter.

I'll bet she doesn't eat dressing on her salads.

"No, I'll bet she doesn't eat salads. She probably eats french fries and bacon cheeseburgers."

Stop whining. Do you want to be beautiful or not? Just because you had a quiet time, you're still a long way from being accepted. You didn't even memorize any Scripture verses today!

Kathy sighed. It was going to be a really long day. It seemed to her that the voice of someone she had come to call the Coach was speaking more often. She called the voice "Coach" for lack of a better name. She couldn't call it a "he," although it sometimes sounded male, like her husband or her pastor. Nor could she call it a "she," although it sometimes sounded female, like her mother or her sister. Whichever, it was forever criticizing, critiquing, and correcting.

Kathy headed home. She saw her neighbor at the mailbox. She rolled down her window and shouted at Marjorie, "Are you already a winner?"

Marjorie Williams laughed and waved back at her. Kathy parked in the messy garage and crossed the lawn to speak to Marjorie.

"How's your dad doing?" Kathy knew that Marjorie's dad was having liver problems and she wanted to get an update. "I prayed for him this morning," Kathy told her truthfully. It felt really good to say that. In fact, she felt like she should get a pat on the back from the Coach later, but she knew she would not.

"He's in stable condition. Bill and I are driving up over the weekend to see him," Marjorie answered sadly.

"I'll keep praying," Kathy assured her. Perhaps God would answer her prayer. She hugged Marjorie and walked toward home.

Well, let's see, you told your neighbor you'd pray for her, but that's still a long way from converting her.

"But I've got to go slow with Marjorie. She's not really open to the gospel."

I won't accept anything less than 100 percent from you, and neither will God.

Discouragement began to set in as Kathy walked inside. Why did it always seem to go like this? She unloaded some groceries and looked at the breakfast dishes still in the sink. A general feeling of disgust settled over her. She was doing so much, and yet she felt so bad. She sorted through the day's mail. Her eyes lingered over the church newsletter, stopping on a statistic that shouted, "ONLY 10 PERCENT OF OUR CHURCH MEMBERS ARE ACTIVELY INVOLVED IN OUR PRAYER MINISTRY: WHAT'S YOUR EXCUSE?"

What is your excuse, Kathy? Why don't you have a prayer partner? I bet that's why the pastor doesn't like you. He knows you're not committed enough!

Against her better judgment, Kathy reached for the phone. She called the prayer hotline and signed up to pray with someone at 5:00 A.M. She hung up, feeling good and wretched at the same time. Why did she do things like that? Nonetheless, it was done, and now that she was committed, there was no turning back. *Oh, well,* Kathy decided, *I'd rather burn out than rust out.*

Having settled the matter, she began to prepare dinner. She grabbed a chicken out of the refrigerator, and started washing some vegetables.

Glancing over at the breakfast nook, she noticed one of the girls' vest draped over a chair. It was Katy's. She must have decided at the last minute this morning not to wear it. Kathy made a lot of the girls' clothes and she took pride in that. She had taken smocking classes when they were younger and sewing classes as they got older.

As a mother, Kathy was into everything. She was a room mother for the girls' classes on alternating years, a Brownie supervisor, a carpool organizer, and a swimming coach in the summer.

As a Christian, Kathy was into even more. She taught a Sunday school class, volunteered time in the church office, played on the women's softball team, had the whole youth group over at the house at least once a month, and now she was involved in the prayer ministry. The only thing that came to her mind that she did not do was volunteer for the meals-on-wheels program.

The Coach didn't need a second invitation. *You should be working with meals-on-wheels!*

Kathy felt a tear run down her cheek.

That's what's wrong with you, Kathy Baker, you're lazy. And you're a wimp. Aren't you willing to work for God?

"I'm tired," she whispered, as another tear fell. "I'm so tired."

You're tired? Don't you think Jesus was tired when he hung there on that cross? He gave his all for you and you're tired?

Kathy looked down at the carrots she had cut up for the chicken dish. She let her gaze rest on the knife just long enough to scare herself. "When will these voices stop?" Kathy wiped another tear and wondered how long it would be before she went mad. She was living under a blanket of despair. She constantly battled with the Coach and continuously lived with a vague feeling of disgust with her own life. "When will I get it right? When will I do enough, be enough, have enough?" She looked at the knife again. "O God, help me," Kathy sobbed. "What do I have to do?"

The Coach was silent. No voices spoke to Kathy. The quiet was deafening. She waited, knowing something would happen soon. When the Coach spoke, it would either sound like her mother, her husband, or her pastor, and she was curious to see who it would be this time. She blew her nose and waited.

"Are you going to answer me?" Kathy hated the Coach, but she had gotten used to the voice. The emptiness scared her. It would be better to have the Coach telling her to go read her Bible, or criticizing her for having such stupid thoughts. The nothingness was terrible. "Now the Coach won't even talk to me."

Then a voice came, but it wasn't the Coach. "Why do you hate yourself?" It was a small voice, and so gentle it made Kathy cry harder.

"I don't know; I just do. It feels like I can never do enough."

"For whom?" the gentle voice asked.

"For anybody, for everybody, I don't know. I just try so hard, and I never seem to get anywhere."

"Where do you want to get?"

Kathy realized it the moment He asked it. "I want everyone to like me." Her tears spilled down her cheeks. "But that won't ever happen, will it?"

She did not need an answer. Not only did she

know it would never happen, but if it did happen, it still wouldn't be enough. "My needs are so huge," she confessed honestly. "I want everyone to notice what I do and love me for it. Then I hate them for making me perform."

At that moment, Kathy had a revelation. "My husband, my mother, my pastor, and all my friends could love and accept me, but I would still want more—" she paused, putting the pieces together—"because *I* don't accept me. And I know that if there is one person on this planet who doesn't love me, then I will side with that person, because that's how I feel about myself."

"Can I tell you how *I* feel about you?" the tender voice spoke again.

"Yes," she whispered through her tears. "Yes, please."

PART FOUR

LIVING FREE

God is about grace, not about keeping score. His acceptance and approval are not earned and are not rewards for doing everything right. His forgiveness is more than a second chance to do better next time.

God's love for us is unconditional and eternally free. When our lives and relationships are impacted by that love, we will be set free. We will be set free to love as he loves. We will be set free to give of ourselves to others.

Freedom may feel like wind on our faces. It may look like seeing our true reflection for the first time. It may even smell like a newborn baby. But it is still freedom and it comes only from God.

15

The Wind of the Spirit

This life jacket is too small, he thought. *Too small and too tight.* Lewis loosened the bindings enough to afford a little more ease in breathing. "That's better," he mumbled to himself. He would have simply taken the thing off, except the blasted rules said that when anyone was on the boat, the life jacket had to be on the body. Even if the boat was still tied to the pier. Lewis sighed and continued to scan the horizon, hoping beyond all hope that something, anything, would capture his attention and help him forget how bored he felt.

It was another beautiful day. The days were always beautiful, except for an occasional shower that would blow in and then move on a few minutes later. Lewis had partnered with his friend Kip to buy a sailboat and then lease dock space at an exclusive boating club, known for its beauty and tranquility. The beauty and tranquility were everything the club had advertised, but after so many days, months, and years, it got to be a little much. What was the use of having a boat if you never went anywhere? But the decisions were not made solely by Lewis, and Kip seemed quite content to stay moored at the dock and read about the glories of boating and life on the seas. So Lewis kept his mouth shut and tried to be content.

Lewis could not feel frustrated with Kip for very long. After all, Kip was his friend, and though he was stiff and overly cautious, he had helped Lewis at a time in his life when he desperately needed help. Lewis had met Kip a couple of years ago when Lewis was struggling with depression. He had lost a dream job that would have set him up for life, and the woman he thought he would marry. He turned to comfort in a bottle and the bottle had left him comfortless, too. Broken, penniless, and desperate, Lewis had found in Kip hope and purpose, and a destiny with the sea on a sailboat. Only problem was, they were still tied to the dock.

Every now and then, Kip would get out the

oars and they would paddle around the inlet for the day. Late in the afternoon they would return very frustrated—they had trouble coordinating their efforts—and very tired. Lewis longed to hoist the sail and let the sailboat be powered by the wind, to feel the salty breeze on his face as they hurtled over the open sea.

When he was tired of sitting, he got up and walked mid-ship to find Kip. The man, only one year his senior, was sitting with his feet dangling over the side, book resting on his life jacket, tacky sunglasses at an odd angle on his face, mouth open, snoring in the mid-afternoon sun. Lewis sat down beside him and sighed, secretly hoping to disturb him enough that he would wake up on his own. Kip snorted, and moved, but did not awaken. Lewis sighed again, a little louder. Yes, Kip was his friend, but enough was enough.

Lewis took a deep breath, shut his eyes and mouth tightly, held it for a moment to let the pressure build, and then let loose the most blood-curdling scream he could muster. What happened next could only be described if you were watching it in slow motion. Kip jumped a good two feet in the air, sending his boating book over the side. He lurched to catch the book, and his glasses fell off his face into the path of his huge feet as he danced to steady the rocking boat.

Lewis heard them crunch and pointed to where they had fallen.

"Good grief!" exclaimed Kip, when he found his voice and wits enough to speak without losing anything else overboard. "What'd you do that for?"

"Sorry, Kip," said Lewis, "the boredom just kind of got to me and I couldn't hold it in anymore."

"Well, good grief, you didn't have to scream in my ear. You made me step on my good glasses."

"Actually, you did that all by yourself. But I'm sorry. I'll get you another pair."

Kip eyed Lewis suspiciously. "What's wrong with you?" he asked as he reached over the side of the boat to fish out his book.

"Um, Kip, do you think today we could untie the boat from the dock and raise the sail?"

"Why would we want to do that?" Kip asked skeptically.

"To let the wind fill the sail, that's why."

"Wind? We don't need wind. We've been doing fine for years. Stop complaining."

"I'm not complaining. I was just kind of hoping there was more to sailing than this."

"Hey, we're sailing," Kip replied firmly. "It's just that we're in control. I have a paddle, and I can get anywhere I want to. We don't need the wind." He squeezed the water out of the book he had been reading, relocated his chair beside the railing, and sat down. "Besides, if we let the wind just blow us where it wants, how do we know where we'll end up?"

"I hadn't thought about that," Lewis confessed honestly.

"See? You'd have gotten us lost," Kip snapped, irritated from the harsh glare. "Blast it! Now I can't read because the sun's in my eyes."

"Put your sunglasses on," said Lewis, giggling.

Meanwhile, Kip turned his chair around to face the opposite direction. "That's better," he said to himself. To Lewis, he said, "I'm going to read some more. If I fall asleep, don't disturb me!"

"Okay," said Lewis, as he went again to the back of the boat. "Wish I could sleep." He sighed. "Yeah, Kip, you're right." He muttered to himself, staring out over the water. "You're always right," he growled. "Yeah, it wouldn't be too much fun to be free. Sailing with the wind." He imagined riding the waves beneath a full sail, powered by the incredible ocean winds. "Nope, you're right. We're much better off right here in dead calm." He sighed again. "We're a lot better off just stuck at the pier." Lewis chewed on that for a moment, and then returned to his friend whose eyes were closed, "Hey, Kip!" he yelled.

Kip was startled again, but this time he did not lose any of his belongings to the sea. He slowly turned his head toward Lewis, whose face was now only a few inches from his own. "What do you want this time?"

Lewis did not move away. "It seems like everytime we start to paddle, we have to quit because you get too tired."

"Now wait a minute!" Kip defended himself. "I always pull my load."

"No, you don't. You paddle in one direction, and I paddle in the other. We just go around in big circles and end up right back here in the shallow water. Then you get frustrated and quit."

"I do not," insisted Kip, off-guard. "And what, all of a sudden, is wrong with the shallow water? At least we know where we are. At least we can see the bottom. If we did what you're talking about, we could end up . . . out there . . . God only knows where." Kip pointed toward the open sea as if the Loch Ness monster might surface at any moment.

"Have you ever been out in the deep?"

"No! And I intend to keep it that way! Now be quiet. I'm trying to read." Kip pushed Lewis away from his chair and sat back down.

Lewis eyed the book Kip was holding. "What are you reading today?"

"*How to Be a Great Sailor Without Being Washed Up.*"

"Is it good?" inquired Lewis, which he doubted since it kept putting Kip to sleep.

"You ought to read it sometime. It will give you something to do."

"I'll have to do that," Lewis replied forlornly. He sighed again. "Hey, how do you know what it's like out there in the deep if you've never been out there, huh?"

"I don't have to go out there to know how frightening it would be. I mean, the waves can get high and the storms can blow in without warning."

"But that happens being tied right here to the dock," replied Lewis, knowing he had won that argument.

But Kip didn't give in. "Look, we're just not set up for it, okay?"

Lewis could not believe his ears. "What are you talking about? We have the finest boat in the club; everything is in great condition. Nothing has had any wear and tear whatsoever. What do you mean we're not set up for it?"

"Well, there's no wind. We'll get stuck out there."

"You don't know that."

"Well, something could go wrong."

"I'm ready for it. Look at me. I'm one big life preserver!"

"Don't you make fun of your life preserver," shouted Kip defensively. "God helps those who help themselves."

"No, God helps those who are helpless," Lewis countered.

"Well, there's no reason to give God any more trouble. He's got enough worries in this world without having to rescue you from your own foolishness. I've had enough of this discussion. We have paddles, and we can get anywhere we want by ourselves. So knock off this talk about the wind and being helpless. Go find something to do and leave me alone."

Lewis shuffled to the front of the boat, defeated. "Well, I'm stuck," he fumed. "I don't know what to do. I guess I'll just sit here and rot." He plunked down on the floor in the middle of the boat by the mast.

"How about being quiet while you rot?" called Kip from his chair, eyes already closed again.

"I don't want to," whined Lewis, louder. "I don't want to rot!" he shouted at the sky.

As he scanned the horizon, something caught his eye. It was a sailboat about half a mile away.

"Hey, look," he said to himself. "Look!" he shouted as he stood, loud enough for Kip to hear. "Look at those guys! Look at the way the wind fills their sail!" Lewis began jumping up and down, pointing and shouting at the other boat. "Hey! Ahoy there, mateys! Ahoy there!"

Kip was annoyed. "Be quiet! Don't yell at them!" He motioned to Lewis to sit down. "They obviously don't do things the way we do!"

"Obviously," Lewis replied with more than a trace of sarcasm. He then turned and yelled even louder at the other boat, "Hey! Come back! I want to go with you guys!"

"What are you doing?" Kip screamed, suddenly aware that the boat was lurching from side to side. "Cut it out! You're rocking the boat." Kip tightened his life jacket, growing more fearful as the rocking increased.

Lewis was desperate to gain the other boaters' attention. He waved and yelled louder as they passed by and then disappeared over the horizon. Lewis was crushed. "They left me," he moaned. "They didn't hear me."

Kip was relieved. "Good! Now cut it out and be still, will you?"

Lewis was angry. "That does it!" he said, as he brushed past Kip, marched off to the rear, and began undoing the knots that secured the boat to the dock. "I'm going to untie the ropes."

Panic swept over Kip, and he began to sweat. "No! You can't do that! Don't untie the ropes! Let's talk this over!"

But Lewis was adamant. When he finished untying the ropes, he pushed the boat away from the dock.

"Wait!" Kip pleaded, beside himself with rage and panic. "You don't know what you're doing! You haven't even read this book!"

Lewis ignored Kip and moved to the mast to organize the ropes in preparation for raising the sail. As he worked, he began to sing a song that a group of old sailors had taught him late one night during their first week of membership at the club. He had no trouble remembering the words that had stirred his soul. Now those words rolled from his lips with vigor, "Come all ye young hearties who follow the sea: Yo ho, blow the man down. The wind that's a-blo . . ."

"Stop it!" Kip interrupted. "We can't go anywhere with the boat looking like this. We still have to swab the deck, batten down the hatches, and . . ."

"Raise the sail," interjected Lewis.

"Raise the sail," Kip echoed. "No! We're *not* raising the sail." Kip ran over to Lewis and grabbed him by the collar of his life jacket, hoping to shake some sense into him. "You're crazy! You don't know what you're doing!"

Lewis threw Kip to the floor of the boat, bent over him, and yelled into his face, "I'm freeing us from doing!"

Kip stared into Lewis's face, stunned by the determination and passion that he saw there. Kip grabbed his paddles and held them close to his body, like a mother defending her child. "Well, I like paddling, Lewis. I'm the chief paddler. If we aren't going to paddle, what am I supposed to do?" he whimpered.

"Put your paddles down," Lewis said simply. He grabbed the ropes and began to pull with all his might, slowly raising the sail.

"Do what?" Kip shrieked.

"Let your paddles go." Lewis continued to pull steadily on the ropes, hoisting the sail higher and higher.

"I don't want to. Do you realize you're trusting in something you can't even see?"

"But I know it's there." The sail was almost to the top of the mast now. When it reached its full height Lewis tugged a second rope that allowed the sail to unfurl. It rolled out and instantly filled with the gentle breeze of the ocean wind. "Look at that! Just look at the way it fills the sail!"

Lewis tied off the sail, trimmed it, and ran to handle the rudder to steer them to open water. "Here we go!" Feeling the wind on his face, he smiled and launched into singing once more as the ship moved farther from the dock. "Come all ye young hearties who follow the sea. . . ."

Kip was still hesitant. "Now don't go too fast!"

"Yo ho, blow the man down. . . ."

"I mean it, Lewis! I think we can go back to the dock now!" Kip held tightly to the side.

"The wind that's a blowin' will soon set you free. . . ."

"Lewis, we've never done it this way before!" cried Kip, tightening his grip on his paddles.

"Give me some time to blow the man down." And again, "Come all ye young hearties who follow the sea. . . ."

"This wind feels pretty good," said Kip, smiling in spite of himself. "Yeah, maybe I could just set one paddle down. . . ."

"Yo ho, blow the man down. . . ."

And as they hit the open water, Kip joined Lewis in singing, "The wind that's a blowin' will soon set us free! Give me some time to blow the man down!"

16

The Beloved Ugly Duckling

I read to my little girl every night. I wish I could say that I always look forward to it, but sometimes I'm so tired that I just want to get it over with. Nonetheless, I am committed to the routine. My wife is with Casey all day long while I battle the office, and when I come home there are too many other distractions to get much quality time together, so bedtime has become "our time." I believe it is important, for both of us. We've learned many truths together. We've grown through *Good Night, Moon*, through the adventures of Winnie the Pooh, and last week we started on Hans Christian Andersen.

Casey is seven and a prolific reader. We've

been having our nightly story time for five years. When she was too young to read, I picked the stories and read them to her. However, in the last few years, she has begun to pick the book, and sometimes she reads to me. But from the beginning, she has always followed the story. Occasionally, she has caught me trying to skip pages. "You skipped a page, Daddy," she protests, putting her hand on my arm. I go back and read it the right way, embarrassed. We have learned many truths together—my daughter and I—with guess who learning the most.

My dad died when I was young, and my mother had to work just to support our family. I was left to myself most of the time, and I developed a real love for books. Sometimes, even today, I will have three books going at one time. It thrills me that Casey enjoys reading, and that reading together is something we can share.

So, sometimes after Casey goes to bed, if I am not too sleepy, I will pick up a book and read until I fall asleep. It is no coincidence, I am certain, that last week I picked up a book by Henri Nouwen, called *Life of the Beloved.* It was recommended to me by a colleague, and I started this book the same night that Casey and I began reading "The Ugly Duckling."

The first night I took a turn reading. The book opens with a mother duck sitting on her nest. She is in a secluded spot in the forest somewhere, waiting for her eggs to hatch. When they begin hatching, they all come out of their shells —one by one—and begin to hop around. One of the eggs does not hatch, though, and the mother duck begins to worry. About that time, the all-knowing grandmother duck comes to visit. The mother duck is still sitting on the one egg.

" 'How are you coming along?' " I read, in my best grandmotherly voice.

" 'Fine, but this one egg is taking such a long time, Grandmother. The shell won't crack,' " I answered as the mother duck. (It isn't enough to be a good father. You must be a good actor/ storyteller as well.)

" 'It's a turkey's egg!' " I shouted in Grandmother Duck's voice. " 'I was cheated like that once and I tell you I had no end of trouble and worry with the creature, for they're afraid of the water. Yes, it's a turkey's egg. Just leave it alone and teach the other children to swim.' " I watched a shadow cross Casey's face at the cruelty of Grandmother Duck.

" 'I'll sit on it a little longer,' said Mother Duck." Casey was reassured. I read on:

At last the big egg cracked. "Cheep, cheep!" said the young one and tumbled out. How big and ugly he was! The duck looked down at him. . . .

"Can he be a turkey chick? Well, we shall soon find out. Into the water he shall go, if I have to kick him in myself."

I continued reading as the Duck family made its way back to the barnyard. Casey grew more concerned as all the animals were cruel to the ugly duckling. I concentrated on the best barnyard voices I could muster.

"Does your face hurt?" the goat was asking.

"No," the duckling answered.

"Well, it's killing me! Baa, Baa!"

Mrs. Mouse came over to get a closer look. Squeaky voice for her: "What a monstrous big duckling. None of the others look like that! Squeak!"

"Mooo, Mooo! That beak could bust the barn! Moo!"

"All of the others are very fine-looking, except for this one," the horse whinnied. "It's a pity you can't make him over again."

Then came the snort from the corner, "Hey, Duck, you got a face only your mama could love, and even she is having a little trouble." I added two snorts for the pig and got a giggle from Casey. I always go for the cheap laughs.

"Be quiet!" quacked Mother Duck. "All of you be quiet!"

"I wish the cat would eat him," said Grandmother Duck.

But the barnyard taunting would not stop. We read of how the duckling was bitten, pushed about, and made fun of by all the other animals. The duckling was heartbroken and didn't know which way to turn. He sobbed to himself, choked back his tears, and decided to run away from the duckyard into the cold, bleak marsh.

I closed the book. "That's where we're going to stop for tonight."

Casey had big tears. "Poor little duckling."

"We'll see what happens tomorrow night," I told Casey. We said prayers together, and Casey prayed for the Ugly Duckling and for me. I turned out the light and went to the living room. Sheila was still out with a friend, and I picked up the Nouwen book again and began to read:

"You are the Beloved," and all I hope is that you can hear these words as spoken to you with all the tenderness and force that love can hold. My only desire is to make these words reverberate in every corner of your being— "You are the Beloved." . . . It certainly is not easy to hear that voice in a world filled with voices that shout: "You are no good, you are ugly; you are worthless; you are despicable, you are nobody—unless you can demonstrate the opposite."

I sat in the living room chair. I had read "The Ugly Duckling" to Casey, and now I was reading it to myself in a different form, in my grown-up world. I was glued to Nouwen's book.

Something stirred very deep within me. I have never felt the acceptance and love that I have longed for. It seems that in every aspect of my life, I have been searching. I married Sheila two years after my first marriage ended. I have found incredible happiness in our family, but there is a nagging that never leaves me. It is the feeling that I am not worth anything. On good days, it's mild; on bad days, it is suffocating. I wish I could say that it comes from having a bad family, but I don't think it does. My mother loved me like crazy. It was hard not having a dad, but I always felt love from my mother. But it was never enough to ease the steady stream of my own self-rejection. I read on:

Over the years I have come to realize that the greatest trap in our life is not success, popularity or power, but self-rejection. Success, popularity and power can, indeed, present a great temptation, but their seductive quality often comes from the way they are part of the much larger temptation to self-rejection. When we have come to believe in the voices that call us worthless, and unlovable, then success, popularity and power are easily perceived as attractive solutions.

I stopped reading. How did this man know me? It was almost scary the way he was speaking about my life. I closed the book and went to bed. My thoughts turned to my job and how much I wanted to "get ahead." I constantly find myself thinking about what the next step will be, or how much money I will make. Until now, however, I never even thought that was an indication of how I felt about myself. Just as I was crawling under the covers, I heard Sheila come into the house. I was glad she was home, but I didn't feel like talking. I turned out the light, and pretended I was sleeping, until I was.

Casey was talking a mile a minute at breakfast the next morning. She told Sheila all about the Ugly Duckling and how everybody made fun of him, and how he had run off into the marsh. I sat flipping through the paper, listening, but not letting it be known that I was listening.

My day was a normal one. Hectic, harried, hurried. Amid phone calls and faxes, my mind wandered back over the words I'd read the night before, *You are the Beloved.* Everything in me resisted. *No, you're not!* my mind shouted at me. *If you were the Beloved, you would own this company.* I realized how much I believed that success was my solution to quiet those inner voices. I got home late and Sheila was mad. I ducked past her to Casey's room.

"Wanna see what the Ugly Duckling's doing?"

Casey squealed with delight. She was already in her pajamas, and she crawled up under the covers. She gathered her most trusted stuffed friends around her and prepared to listen.

"How was school today?" I asked as I took the book off the shelf.

"Really fun," she answered. "We got to pet some baby bunnies, and I got to feed the mama. She was white, and the babies were spotty, and really soft."

I took my place beside her on the bed, and opened the book. "Where were we?"

"The Ugly Duckling had run away," Casey reminded me.

"Oh, yes," I said as I turned to the page. "Here we are."

He was so tired and miserable that he stayed there . . . two whole days. . . . Then two wild geese came, or rather two wild ganders. They were not long out of the shell and therefore rather pert.

I added a few honks, and turned the page.

"I say, comrade," they said, "you are so ugly that we have taken quite a fancy to you! Will you join us and be a bird of passage? There is another marsh close by, and there are some charming wild geese there. All are sweet young ladies who can say quack! You are ugly enough to make your fortune among them." Just at that moment, bang! bang! was heard up above, and both the wild geese fell dead among the reeds, and the water turned blood red. Bang! Bang! went the guns, and whole flocks of wild geese flew up from the rushes and the shots peppered among them again. . . . The retrieving dogs wandered about in the swamp— splash! splash! . . . It was terribly alarming to the poor duckling. . . . Just at that moment a frightful big dog appeared close beside him. His tongue hung right out of his mouth and his eyes glared wickedly. He opened his great chasm of a mouth close to the duckling, showed his sharp teeth and—splash!—went on without touching him.

"Oh, thank Heaven!" sighed the duckling. "I am so ugly that even the dog won't bite me!"

Casey laughed. I laughed, too. I read on:

He hurried away from the marsh as fast as he could. . . . Towards night he reached a poor little cottage. It was such a miserable hovel that it remained standing only because it could not make up its mind which way to fall. . . . An old woman lived there with her cat and her hen.

The cat, however, was the master of this house, and the hen, its mistress.

"Can you lay eggs?" asked the hen.

"I don't think so," replied the duckling.

"Can you arch your back, purr, or give off sparks?" asked the cat who could do all of the above. However, he could only give off sparks when someone rubbed his fur the wrong way.

"No," answered the duckling who was sitting in the corner alone. Then he began to think of the fresh air and sunshine, and an uncontrollable longing seized him. He wanted desperately to float on the water. At last he could not help telling the hen.

"What on earth possesses you?" she asked. "You have nothing to do. . . . Lay some eggs or take to purring, and you will get over it."

"But it is so delicious to float on the water," said the duckling. "It is so delicious to feel it rushing over your head when you dive to the bottom."

"That would be a fine amusement!" said the hen. "I think you have gone mad! Ask the cat about it. He is the wisest creature I know. Ask him if he is fond of floating on the water or diving under it. . . ."

"You do not understand me," said the duckling.

"Well, if we don't understand you, who should? I suppose you don't consider yourself cleverer than the cat . . . not to mention me! Don't make a fool of yourself, child, and thank your stars for all the good we have done you. . . . But you are an idiot, and there is no pleasure in associating with you. . . ."

So away went the duckling. He floated on the water and ducked underneath it, but he was looked askance at and slighted by every living creature for his ugliness. . . .

Then one evening, the sun was just setting in wintry splendor . . ."

I looked down at Casey, whose eyelids were like sandbags. "Let's stop here, okay? We'll finish it tomorrow night."

"But I want to know what happens," she answered sadly.

"I do, too, and we'll find out tomorrow." I kissed her forehead and turned out her light. She was asleep in seconds. But not me.

I padded to the living room. I should have put the book back on her shelf, but I was still holding it in my hand. It would not be fair to finish it without Casey, but I really had forgotten the way it ended, and I wanted to find out. Besides, I rationalized to myself, I would read it better if I was familiar with it. I exercised my will power, and instead of continuing with the duckling, I picked up Henri Nouwen and found my place in *Life of the Beloved.*

Though the experience of being the Beloved has never been completely absent from my life, I never claimed it as my core truth. I kept running around it in large or small circles, always looking for someone or something able to convince me of my Belovedness. It was as if I kept refusing to hear the voice that speaks from the very depth of my being and says: "You are my Beloved, on you my favor rests." That voice has always been there, but it seems that I was much more eager to listen to other, louder voices saying: "Prove that you are worth something; do something relevant, spectacular or powerful, and then you will earn the love you so desire." Meanwhile, the soft, gentle voice that speaks in the silence and solitude of my heart remained unheard or, at least, unconvincing.

I read it in the words of a nineteenth-century storyteller, and again in the words of an Ivy League theology professor: You have a choice to believe what is true about you or to believe what others say is true about you. I could hear the "cat" and the "hen" of my grown-up world cackling constantly. "Can you prove to us that you are worth something?" or, "You're divorced? Well, nothing else you have to offer society will matter.

You certainly aren't the Beloved of God after that kind of thing." It is so easy for me to listen to those voices because I really believe them. Not only might I hear others say those things, I tell myself those things.

Sheila came into the living room where I was sitting. "Are you still mad at me?" I asked sheepishly.

"Nope, because you're home. I only get mad at you when you're not home and I feel abandoned by you." Her feelings seemed to flow so freely, whereas my feelings seemed to get clogged in the drain. She continued, "Thanks for reading to Casey. I peeked in on you guys, and she was thoroughly engrossed." She smiled a winning smile.

"What are you reading?" Sheila leaned over to catch a glimpse of the title. *Life of the Beloved?* She looked at me. "Is it good?"

"It's very good." I resisted telling her about "The Ugly Duckling" and the way both stories were speaking to my soul at the same time. Instead, I just said, "You should read it when I get finished." I don't know why I find it so hard to talk about my feelings. I want to tell her how I feel about myself, how much I love her and admire her, but the words just won't come out.

Sheila got up and went to the kitchen, and I resumed my reading.

Becoming the Beloved means letting the truth of our Belovedness become enfleshed in everything we think, say or do. It entails a long and painful process of appropriation or, better, incarnation. As long as "being the Beloved" is little more than a beautiful thought or a lofty idea that hangs above my life to keep me from becoming depressed, nothing really changes. What is required is to become the Beloved in the commonplaces of my daily existence and, bit by bit, to close the gap that exists between what I know myself to be and the countless specific realities of everyday life.

I sat in my chair for a couple more hours that night, long after Sheila had gone to bed, and I analyzed my life. Going through a divorce—even the death of my mother—had not prompted me to look at my life as deeply as I did on this night. Somehow I could see so much more clearly. I could see how rarely I thought of myself in any positive light. I saw how I always weighed my achievements against the achievements of others. Most importantly, I saw how not seeing myself as the Beloved was ruining and robbing my life. But my doubts would not leave me. Am I really the Beloved? Does God care for me in a way that I do not care for myself?

I couldn't sleep. I lay in my bed until 2:30 A.M. with those questions rolling around in my head. What would my life look like if I believed I was beloved of God? Could I ever believe it? Is my mind playing tricks on me? Would I begin to believe that I am beloved, only to find out that I'm really not, and Henri Nouwen didn't know what he was writing about? I dreamed short dreams. Most of my dreams were about ducks, and in one recurring scene, I was running wildly around the barnyard, screaming. About 5:30 A.M., I awoke for good. I knew that I wouldn't be sleeping anymore. I put the coffee on and went to the living room so I wouldn't disturb Sheila. The Hans Christian Andersen book was still by my chair, and I sat down. I opened the book.

The reading went much faster silently. I found where I had left off with Casey, and I continued reading:

One evening the sun was just setting in wintry splendor when a flock of beautiful large birds appeared out of the bushes. The duckling had never seen anything so beautiful. They were dazzlingly white with long waving necks. They were swans, and uttering a peculiar cry they spread out their magnificent broad wings and flew away from the cold regions to warmer lands and open seas. . . . The ugly little duckling became strangely uneasy. He circled round and round in the water like a wheel, craning his neck up into the air after them. Then he uttered a shriek so piercing and so strange that he was quite frightened by it himself. Oh, he could not forget those beautiful birds, those happy birds. . . .

But it would be too sad to mention all the privation and misery he had to go through during the hard winter. When the sun began to shine warmly again, the duckling was in the marsh, lying among the rushes. The larks were singing and the beautiful spring had come.

Then all at once he raised his wings and they flapped with much greater strength than before and bore him off vigorously. Before he knew where he was, he found himself in a large garden where the apple trees were in full blossom and the air was scented with lilacs. . . .

Just in front of him he saw three beautiful white swans advancing towards him from a thicket. . . . The duckling recognized the majestic birds, and he was overcome by a strange melancholy.

"I will fly to them, the royal birds, and they will hack me to pieces because I, who am so ugly, venture to approach them. But it won't matter!" . . .

So he flew into the water and swam towards the stately swans. They saw him and darted towards him with ruffled feathers.

"Kill me!" said the poor creature, and he bowed his head towards the water and awaited his death. But what did he see reflected in the transparent water?

He saw below him his own image, but he was no longer a clumsy dark gray bird, ugly and ungainly. He was himself a swan!

I could imagine hearing him trumpet, "I'm a swan, I'm a swan, I'm a swaaan!"

The big swans swam round and round him and stroked him with their bills.

Some little children came into the garden with corn and pieces of bread which they threw into the water, and the smallest one cried out, "There is a new one!" The other children shouted with joy, "Yes, a new one has come." And they clapped their hands and danced about. . . . "The new one is the prettiest of them all. He is so young and handsome." And the old swans bent their heads and did homage before him. . . .

He rustled his feathers and raised his slender neck aloft, saying with exultation in his heart, "I never dreamt of so much happiness when I was the Ugly Duckling!"

I closed the book. A tear ran down my cheek as I pondered the simplicity of the message. Born in a duckyard, he thought he was a duck. But he knew something was wrong. He wasn't a duck at all, but a swan. He just didn't know it.

The implications were so clear for my own life. God was calling me his Beloved, and I kept looking around the duckyard to see if it was true. If I could find some real confirmation that I had worth, maybe I could believe it. But confirmation never comes from the duckyard. Success is always "just around the next corner," so I stay on the treadmill. I have worked too hard, spent too much and compromised my last principle trying to bring myself a sense of worth that will never come from the duckyard.

In the quiet marsh of my own soul, I caught a glimpse of who I really am: A Swan, the Beloved of God. It would be so much easier for me to accept that God could never love me than to accept that I am his Beloved. *Please help me* was all I could think of to pray. I reached for *Life of the Beloved,* and once again I heard God speaking to me from its pages.

> The change of which I speak is the change from living life as a painful test to *prove* that you deserve to be loved, to living it as an unceasing *"Yes"* to the truth of that Belovedness. Put simply, life is a God-given opportunity to become who we are, to affirm our own true spiritual nature, claim our truth, appropriate and integrate the reality of our being, but, most of all, to say "Yes" to the One who calls us the Beloved.

Casey and I are still reading together. She forgave me for reading ahead in "The Ugly Duckling." Sheila read *Life of the Beloved* and we have had some wonderful talks. I still work too much, and on occasion, I forget or I ignore what is true about me. But it is rare for me to miss a special time that I set aside almost every morning to be very still and very quiet and to say "Yes" to the voice that calls me his Beloved.

17

Scripts

We stared out at a room full of couples. Nervously, I said, "Hi, we're the Randolphs, and we have scripts." The whole room nodded supportively. "Hi, Randolphs." Although we had been a part of this support group for months, this was the first time we had ever told our story.

"My name is Catherine, and this is my husband Brian. We've known for quite some time that we had scripts, we just didn't want to acknowledge it. We were scared." That brought smiles and looks of encouragement.

"One night a year or so ago," Brian continued, "we were fighting the kids' script." There were more nods from the audience. "And it hit both of us that we'd had this argument before. We stood there staring at each other with this overwhelming sense of *déjà vu.*"

I jumped in to continue the story. "I told him, 'We have fought this fight before.' He said to me, 'No, we've fought this fight *many* times before.' This is the 'Aha!' moment for people who have scripts. If you don't have that 'We've-been-here-before' moment, you either don't have scripts or you don't know that you have scripts." The crowd agreed, and applauded.

"So," Brian continued, "although we didn't do anything about it at that time, we were aware of it. Over the next few months, we noticed five scripts that began to surface." A deep "ooh," arose from the crowd. "Five scripts were pretty serious. And three, of course, were the biggies: Money, Kids, and Sex. We were powerless to do anything about them, but we knew they were there."

"We actually tried to deny it for a while," I explained. There was laughter of identification throughout the room. "When we'd argue, we'd try not to use our scripts. We'd even argue about something unrelated so we wouldn't be tempted to come back to our scripts. Crazy, I know."

"The more we tried not to use them," Brian went on, "the more they flowed from our mouths.

We were fighting like cats and dogs every day. There was hardly anything either of us could say that didn't trigger one of our scripts. Then one day, Catherine said to me—" he quivered a little as he recounted that day—" 'I can't live like this anymore.' We were stuck and I knew it, but I didn't have a clue of what to do about it. So I did nothing. I actually heard her cry out, but I had no life jacket to throw her, so I just stayed busy on the boat. At which point we stopped talking altogether, which is really a script, too. Even though there were no words, there was a lot of communication going on."

"Brian was right. I felt like I was drowning." The audience had grown respectfully silent in the face of the seriousness of our situation. "I knew we needed help, but I was afraid that he didn't want things to change."

"Oh, I wanted things to change," Brian interjected. "I just thought she was looking to me to be the one to change them, and I had no idea how to do that. I was scared to death, too."

"So there we were, surviving from day to day," I continued. "And who calls us up to see if we want to have dinner but Jim and Melanie Green!" Uproarious laughter filled the room at the mention of Jim and Melanie—the outspoken couple of this group. At this, everyone clapped and whistled, and I asked Jim and Melanie to stand, and the audience clapped even more. Finally the room settled down, and I continued our story.

"We were halfway through dinner—actually having a wonderful time—when they started talking about how their marriage had been revolutionized. Well, I felt myself starting to slip into depression." Another big laugh. "Except Melanie didn't go into the usual I-meet-him-at-the-door-now-in-Saran-wrap speech. She started talking about how they were in a process of tearing up their old 'scripts.' We had never heard the word *scripts* used in terms of the way we argued or played out our conflicts, but the minute she said it, we knew exactly what it was. And we knew we had the same trouble. 'Scripts,' Jim explained to us, 'are those "little plays" that we use in marriage. You know, like the garbage script.' "

Brian interrupted. "Like when she says, 'Could you take out the garbage?' And I say, 'Yes, but can I do it later?' Is that a script? And he said, 'Without a doubt.' "

I continued, "So I asked Melanie, 'What about the part where he never does it? Is that part of the script, too?' I remember Brian glared at me. And Melanie said, 'Yes, and then that usually brings on the You-Never/I-Always script, perhaps followed by the You-Think-You-Are-So-

Good/I-Am-So-Bad script.' We understood this concept. Although we didn't talk with them much more about it that night, I felt like someone knew where we were. Brian must have felt that way, too, because the next day I called Melanie and Brian called Jim. We poured out our hearts individually, neither one of us knowing that the other was doing the same. The following week we sat right back over there in that corner of this room." The crowd broke out in loud, thunderous applause.

Brian cleared his throat. "I guess at this point we are supposed to share with you our scripts." The audience got very quiet. This was the most personal aspect of the evening, when members of the group share their experiences. We had decided to share three. This is our Money Script:

Brian: We just don't have the money.

Catherine: Yes, we do.

Brian: Why aren't you ever satisfied with
            what we have? Why do you always
            want more?

Catherine: More food? Maybe more clothes, a
            few houseplants? You're right, I'm
            so extravagant.

Brian: Why can't I say no to you?

Catherine:	You can. You're doing it right now. You're absolutely great at it!
Brian:	You would spend every last dime we had.
Catherine:	You're wrong. I could never pry it out of your clenched fist!
Brian:	You're just not practical.
Catherine:	And you're not fun.

"And on good days, we would leave it at that," I said. "We would see each other as the enemy who was holding us back from what we really wanted. A lot of our money script came from our parents' money script. But we didn't know that until we began to talk to each other about it."

Brian said, "I must have heard my dad say a hundred times to my mother: 'You're just not practical.' So I said it to Catherine. The truth is, she is practical. Not all of the time, nor as much as I am. But our script was set, and we very rarely strayed from our tried-and-true arguments."

"Don't misunderstand," I tried to clarify. "They don't always look exactly the same, but they are. They begin in a myriad of ways. Brian could be out mowing the lawn, come in to get some water, and step on a Lego. He would then yell at Timothy for leaving it on the floor.

Timmy would cry and run to his room, which would prompt me to start the Kids' Script:

Catherine: Why do you speak to him like that?

Brian: Like what?

Catherine: Like he can't do anything right.

Brian: I didn't speak to him like that.

Catherine: You don't know how you come across.

Brian: And I guess you are going to tell me how I come across.

Catherine: You should just be more gentle with him.

Brian: Like you are?

Catherine: I didn't say that.

Brian: You might as well have. I don't want to treat him like you treat him. I am his father, you are his mother.

Catherine: He needs more from you.

Brian: When did you become such a parenting expert?

Catherine: When you became such a rotten parent.

"I said some awful things," I confessed. "I know that's a part of having scripts, but it is still terrible. The more the scripts reinforce your own opinion, the more the other person becomes the bad guy. The more I saw him as hard on the kids, the more it pushed me to be soft. Whenever a difficult situation arose where a decision had to be made, we didn't have to think about it. We both went to our corners. He said no and I said yes."

"It put me in the role as the bad guy with the kids, too, and that was really hard." He squeezed my hand. I squeezed back.

"One more script," I said, "and this one is certainly the toughest one to share. This is the Sex Script:

Brian:	Why not?
Catherine:	Because I'm not "in the mood."
Brian:	You're never in the mood.
Catherine:	You're never *not* in the mood. I'm just tired and I don't want to.
Brian:	Fine.
Catherine:	Now you're mad.
Brian:	No, I'm not.
Catherine:	Yes, you are. I can tell, because you're not even holding my hand.
Brian:	Well, you don't want to have sex.

Catherine:	Just because I don't want to have sex doesn't mean you can't hold my hand. But you don't want to hold my hand because it's not going to lead anywhere.
Brian:	That's not true.
Catherine:	Yes, it is. If you don't see the end result, it's not worth your effort.
Brian:	C'mon, how long has it been?
Catherine:	I don't know.
Brian:	Three weeks, four days, five hours, and (checks watch) fourteen minutes.
Catherine:	Good grief.
Brian:	See, you don't know. What does that say about you?
Catherine:	That I'm not preoccupied.
Brian:	Preoccupied? You're not even post-occupied. You're so unoccupied, it's not even funny.
Catherine:	Well, I have a lot to do.
Brian:	Like I don't?
Catherine:	I just don't seem to have time!
Brian:	Once a month? You bathe the dog more often than that.
Catherine:	I enjoy bathing the dog.
Brian:	What?
Catherine:	I didn't mean it like that. . . .

Brian:	You don't enjoy having sex with me?
Catherine:	I didn't say that.
Brian:	Yes, you did.
Catherine:	I was trying to be cute about bathing the dog and it came out wrong. I'm sorry.
Brian:	There's a little bit of truth in every joke.
Catherine:	Even the jokes you make about my weight? You see? I feel like you think I'm fat!
Brian:	Honey . . .
Catherine:	Don't start! And you wonder why I don't want to take my clothes off?
Brian:	Honey, I'm fat, too.
Catherine:	Darn right you are—but it doesn't seem to bother you. Leave me alone.
Brian:	Fine.
Catherine:	Fine.

Brian paused for a moment, looked at me, and then spoke to the audience. "We stand before you today to confess our desire that our scripts be torn up and thrown into the trash can!" Wild applause broke out. Brian continued to speak clearly and boldly. "We want to deal with our issues as they come up, and we want to live in the present. We don't want the scripts that our parents wrote and played out to be played out yet again in our own household. We don't want the scripts that the culture has written to have any place in our marriage. And, most of all, we want to stop writing scripts ourselves. We don't want to go to the filing cabinet anymore and pull out Money Script #103. That serves no function for us but to keep us in a perpetual argument mode.

"People can change and God is merciful to show us how. Apart from God's love and grace, we'd be stuck with these scripts. We'd merely react to each other rather than take any positive action. After a while, our scripts would become so well-rehearsed that we'd be saying our lines like broken records while our marriage shriveled up and died. We are hoping and praying for something more than that."

Brian kissed my cheek. He took the three scripts that we had read and tore them in half in front of the audience. Then he tore the halves in half again. The audience was on their feet. We stepped down from the stage to a standing ovation.

18

Shameless Persistence

anic. It was my turn to lead the Bible study for our weekly small group session. Of the six couples in our group, my turn came around every twelve weeks. During the interim, I felt good for about six weeks; stress began to build for three; then outright panic set in for the last two. I hated teaching, or more accurately, I hated preparation. No, I hated teaching, too. Everyone was positive and affirming afterward, but I rarely felt my lesson connected. My ultimate goal was to get through it.

We were in the middle of a series on the life practices of Christians and my assignment was prayer. I groaned internally. I knew prayer was important, but it wasn't something I did regularly. I rarely found time each day to speak with my wife, much less to God.

So how was I to teach on prayer? Well, I began by locating through my Bible computer program all of the references to prayer. There were lots, especially in the New Testament, though most of the references were simple exhortations to pray. Not much on how or why. The biggest reference came in the eleventh chapter of Luke, where Jesus recited the Lord's Prayer and then taught on the subject. So I dove in and found some interesting morsels of truth. Here's how my lesson went:

And it came about one day while Jesus was praying, that some of his disciples asked him to teach them how to pray. They were quite concerned. John the Baptizer had already taught his disciples to pray and, well, they walked around praying a lot, and one might think Jesus' disciples were feeling a little left out. "So teach us to pray," they asked.

Jesus was quite willing to oblige.

"Our Father," he instructed them to begin.

Did he really mean we could call God "Dad?"

"Which art in heaven,"

Not a reflection of our earthly fathers, but the Perfection of everything we have ever longed for a father to be.

"Hallowed be thy name."

Revered, sacred, holy, divine.

"Give us day by day our daily bread."

Father, give us that food which will keep our bodies and souls alive.

"And forgive us our sins; for we also forgive every one that is indebted to us."

You died to clear our debt. We will die to ourselves to clear the debts of others.

"And lead us not into temptation;"

We are so tempted to believe that by bigger, better, more aggressive, more persistent living, we can have life.

"But deliver us from evil, and show us the everlasting way. Amen."

Save us from ourselves and from this broken world, and reveal to us the way of your truth.

After Jesus had given them what we call "The Lord's Prayer," he told them a parable. Now don't decide too quickly what he wanted to show them. If he wanted to come right out and tell them something, why would he tell a story?

Jesus said something like this: Suppose you have a friend. And suppose you go to your friend at midnight. Of course, your friend would not consider you a friend for very long if you made a habit of coming to him at midnight. As it is, being hailed at midnight, even once, is not very endearing. I'm sure Peter spoke up to say that if he had a friend who woke him up from a sound sleep, that friend would then have dental problems.

But let's say you had to go to your friend at midnight because you had another friend come to you late in the night who needed a place to stay and some food to eat. Being a little grumpy yourself, you mumble something unintelligible, and let the person come in because it's dark out and cold, and there's no sense arguing because you're not going to turn someone away in the middle of the night. You point out the couch, the bathroom, the clean towels, the blankets, and tell your friend that it's good to see him and that you'll catch him in the morning.

Now before you can turn around, your friend asks for something to eat before retiring. It seems he is a little low on cash and has not eaten anything all day. So you say, "No problem. I've got some fresh bread in the pantry. Help yourself." But your friend says, "Where's the pantry?" You sigh, go to the kitchen, yourself, open the pantry door. Lo and behold, no bread. You ate it all for dinner. And even gave some of the crumbs to your dog.

What do you do? Your friend needs something to eat. It's too late for pizza delivery and the store is closed. You have no choice. You grab your coat and slippers, get into your car, and drive to your other friend's house, hoping beyond all hope that he is still up. And, of course, as you pull into the driveway, the house is dark. Quiet. Everyone is sound asleep. You want to go home. You hate being in this situation. Quick, turn off the car lights before you disturb someone. And don't slam the car door. Now you stand outside the door of the house for a few seconds, not wanting to ring the doorbell, but knowing you have no other choice. You wish bread would simply pop out of thin air so you wouldn't have to bother anyone.

You ring the doorbell. Nothing happens. You wait. Still nothing. You ring the doorbell again. The dog barks. Oh, no! Now you've disturbed the whole household.

"Who is it?" comes your friend's voice over the intercom.

"It's me," you answer apologetically.

"Who's 'me'?"

"Your friend."

"I don't have any friends who wake me up in the middle of the night."

"Listen, I'm really sorry about this, pal, but I need a loaf of bread. I know you have it. Can you spare me some?"

There is a long pause.

"Are you there?" You ring the doorbell again. The dog barks, again.

"Don't do that anymore," your friend says. "You'll wake up the kids, then I'll be in for it."

"But I have a friend who has come in from out of town unexpectedly. He needed a place to stay and something to eat, and I'm out of food and the store is closed and you know how it is," you finish weakly.

Silence.

"Hello?"

"If I get up, I'll disturb my wife."

"I know, and I'm sorry."

"Come back in the morning."

"My guest is hungry and he's had a really hard day. . . ."

"Well, so have I. Listen, stop bothering me. The door is locked, the alarm is set, my family is asleep with me, and I can't get up without disturbing the whole house. Go away."

At this point, you are desperate. "Look, I just need one measly loaf of bread." You feel your temperature rising. "I'll bring you back *ten* loaves of bread tomorrow."

"No. Go away."

"Go away?" You start yelling. "Go away? I need one loaf of bread and you're practically the

Sunbeam plant, and you're telling me to go
away?"

Silence.

"I'm sorry I yelled at you," you say politely,
but in your heart, you are still yelling. "You're
right; it's an inconvenience. I wish I didn't have
to bother you or your family, but I have no other
options."

Silence.

"I'm just going to wait. I'll be right out here.
No, I'm going to keep ringing the doorbell while
I wait. I might even honk the car horn if I get
good and brave! But I'm not leaving. Because I
don't have anywhere else to go. Do you hear me?
No other options. My only hope is you."

Jesus said that though the friend would not get
up simply because of his friendship with the man
at the door, he did get up because his friend was
bold and shameless and persistent. And he gave
his friend as much as he needed.

My small group applauded. Probably for my acting ability. I continued speaking, "I think Jesus
was trying to say to the disciples that prayer
wasn't so much a plan of action as a state of
being. It is a desperate dependence on God. A
shameless pursuit of the One, the only One, who
can touch the needs that exist at the core of our

beings. All of them. At any moment. Jesus calls us his friends, and he finishes by saying that if we who are broken and sinful know what good gifts are and how to give them, shouldn't our heavenly Father who is Perfect and Truly Good know even more how to do so?"

I closed with this poem:

Shameless persistence
Is not just persistence
Not trying harder
Not repeated knocking with vain babble.
Shameless persistence
Is going on,
Resolutely, stubbornly
In spite of the humiliation, and the disgrace of being
*   needy.*
Out of sheer desperation
We turn to our Father.
But that's embarrassing!
That's just not reasonable
Nor respectable.
I'm sorry, the door is locked.
My children and I are in bed.
I will not get up and give you back the life you are
*   so desperately clinging to.*
But let go of your life,

Offer me a shameless acceptance of your death in
  Christ,
And then,
Ask . . .
And it shall be given.
Seek . . .
And you will find.
Knock . . .
And I will open the door.
Father, my only hope is you.
The heart of prayer.

The Bible study was over. My small group was silent. And I had twelve weeks before my next turn.

19

Baby

I'll never forget the day she told me. She walked into my bedroom, her face swollen from crying. She was white as a ghost and she was trembling. I knew immediately something bad had happened. She looked me in the eye only once, and tears spilled down her cheeks.

She couldn't speak, so I began to ask the just-nod-if-that's-it questions. "Did someone die?" *No.* "Is someone hurt?" She hesitated and nodded yes. I think I knew then that something had happened to Sarah. I cupped her face in my hands and looked her in the eyes, "Are you okay?" She shook her head no and began to sob again.

I grabbed her and held her for dear life. I don't know how mothers know these things, but they just do. My little girl was pregnant. A wave of nausea crashed down, my head started to spin, and I felt my knees buckle. "Let's sit down," I whispered. We moved as one toward the edge of my bed.

Nothing had prepared me to deal with this moment in my life. Dan, my husband, and I had been having our own problems. Financially we were struggling, and now my daughter was pregnant. I was drowning. Emotions danced around me—anger, disappointment, despair, rage, pity. How would I respond?

Now it was my turn to look away. My daughter's eyes searched for mine and I hid them from her. What would I say? I thought about abortion, and my body shuddered. I pictured little Sarah on a cold stainless steel table, and my tears fell like a waterfall. I took a deep breath and glanced over at my daughter. She looked so scared.

"I'm sorry, Mom," she cried as she buried her head into my chest once more.

What if she hadn't come to me? What if she had been too afraid and tried to take care of everything on her own? I held on to her tightly. My resolve was established. She had come to me for help and I would help her.

In that moment I saw more than I wanted to see. I saw how far apart we had all grown. I saw how we had abandoned our faith. I saw how much I had been working and how much Jim had been gone. I saw Sarah trying to find security outside of our family. My gaze found hers. "I'm sorry, Sarah. Can you forgive me?" She looked puzzled. "I've been working so much. I haven't been here for you. I had no idea things had gone so far."

"It's my fault," she said.

I realized that my daughter knew more than I thought she knew. I dropped her off at church, feeling good that she was running with the right crowd. Now I felt stupid and selfish. I was so blind. Her body had changed and boys were calling her, but we had never talked about sex. The pain set in like a dull ache. I had failure stamped on my mother résumé.

"I knew you didn't want me to date Cody," she confessed.

"Cody?" I felt worse.

"Yes."

Cody was every mother's nightmare. He came to pick up Sarah for a dance about a month ago. When he pulled into the driveway and honked the horn, I walked out to meet him. Dan was out of town, so I told Cody, in no uncertain terms, that he would park his car and ring the doorbell if he wanted a date with my daughter for the dance. Of course, Sarah watched from the window with horror. Cody came to the door for Sarah, but he wasn't happy, nor was I. After the dance, I never thought they had gone out again. Apparently, they had. "Oh, Sarah." I put my head in my hands. "Does Cody know?"

Sarah hung her head, and I listened in absolute pain as my daughter replayed their conversation.

He didn't wait for her after class like he usually did. She saw him walking toward his car, and she yelled across the student parking lot. "Hey, Cody, wait up." She started walking fast. "Hey, Cody." She was out of breath as she reached him. "Why didn't you wait for me after class?"

He opened his car door, slid into the driver's seat of an old Ford Mustang, and stared at the wheel.

She tried to read his face. "What's wrong?"

"Nothing."

"Why are you acting this way?"

"What way?" His gaze shifted to the ashtray.

"Like you can't stand me." She paused. "What's wrong?"

For the first time, Cody looked at her directly. "What's wrong with *you?*"

"N—nothing," she stuttered. "Why?"

"That's not what Colette said."

Sarah felt her face flush with heat. "What did Colette say?"

Cody looked back at the steering wheel. "Nothing."

She had to know. Colette was one of her best friends, but she had a really big mouth. "What did Colette say?"

"She said you bought one of those home deals." His eyes never left the wheel.

"She said *what?*" All of the color drained from Sarah's face. *How could Colette do this to me?* she thought.

"She said you took a pregnancy test," he stated flatly. "Is it true?" He rolled his eyes from the wheel up to Sarah. "I guess you weren't gonna tell me."

"I didn't think I would have to," she said. She felt naked standing there in the parking lot. Other students continued to walk by and casually stare. She wished she was anywhere but here.

"Well?" Cody was waiting for her to say something.

"Well, what?" Sarah felt a sting at her eyes. *Not now, don't cry.*

"Is there something you need to tell me?" he asked arrogantly.

"I don't know, Cody. Is there something you need to tell me?" she shot back.

"What do you mean?"

"Well, with you walking off like you can't stand me, the answer is pretty clear."

"I was just mad about finding out from Colette that you got one of those tests."

"Yeah, I'm pretty mad at Colette about that, too." It was Sarah's turn to look at the ground. No telling how long she stood there.

"Are you pregnant?" The question cut like a knife.

"Are you breaking up with me?" Her tears fell on the pavement. It seemed like it took Cody forever to answer. But Sarah could not look at him.

"It depends on your answer to my question," he said finally, matter-of-factly. How could she ever have cared for him? Her tears fell faster. He quickly followed up, "It hasn't been that great between us lately. I mean, your parents hate me. I was gonna say . . . maybe we should date other people."

"Cody, wait," Sarah pleaded.

"I can't marry you, Sarah! I can't date a girl that's pregnant. I can't; I just can't. I mean, I care about you and all, but . . . I can't drop out of school and work. I couldn't play football."

She couldn't believe her ears. "What?"

"If I don't play, I lose my chance at a scholarship. Coach would kill me. . . . I could never throw my life away like that!" He slammed the steering wheel with his fist and stole a glance in her direction. "And it's not just that. I mean, I'm not ready to settle down. I've got my whole life ahead of me."

It seemed so clear to her now. *He doesn't care about you, Sarah. Stop fooling yourself.* Why wasn't it that clear the night they did it? How could he just walk away? This was getting harder for Sarah by the minute. "What am I supposed to do, huh? I can't just run home and tell my family, and I can't exactly hide it from anybody."

"You could get an abortion." Just like that, it came out of his mouth.

"I know that. Don't you think I know that? I don't know what I'm gonna do." Sarah fought for control. She wanted to run away and hide. How did she get in so deep, so fast? She felt a long way from home.

"You gotta do what's best for you." Cody's words sounded as tender as a jackhammer to her soul. "I hope you make the right decision." He reached over to shut his Mustang door.

"Cody, wait."

He slammed the door. "I can't help you, Sarah." He started the car.

"I thought you loved me," she sobbed over the engine noise.

"I really thought I did." He turned on the radio. "I'm sorry."

Sarah shouted for the first time. "You're sorry? I'm pregnant . . . and you're sorry?"

"I'll pay for the abortion." He put the car in drive.

If she was unsure before, she wasn't anymore. "I'm not going to have an abortion." She turned away. Now it was Cody's turn to pursue.

"Sarah, come on. What other choice do you have?"

"I don't know." She started walking.

He pulled alongside her in the Mustang, "What are you gonna tell your folks?"

She kept walking. "I guess I'll tell them they were right about you."

Just as she finished the story, we heard the garage door going up. We sat in frozen silence like people who think they hear a burglar. Sarah glanced at the clock on my bedside table, and her eyes told all. "What am I gonna tell Daddy?" She cried harder.

"The truth, honey. He loves you. I know it's hard, but he needs to know." A thousand thoughts ran through my head. *Let's get the hardest part over with, and then we'll deal with the fallout.* I was lost in my thoughts when Sarah got up.

"I'll be right back." She left the bedroom, and I wasn't sure if I should go meet Dan or wait until she came back. It turned out that I didn't have to make that decision. Sarah didn't come back to my room; she went to the living room to talk to her daddy.

He was sitting in the recliner reading the paper. It usually takes him about thirty seconds after coming home to assume that position. In the past few years, with me working and all the kids out of the house except Sarah, he'd had more opportunity to sit and read. Rarely did he miss the opportunity.

"Hi, Dad." Sarah was probably trying to get it over with before she chickened out. If nothing else, my daughter has guts.

"Hello, sweetheart," he said, from behind the paper.

"Um, how's work?" She picked the chair farthest from him and sat down.

"Fine," said the paper. "How's school?" They both knew their parts. Getting the conversation beyond work and school would be quite a challenge.

"Okay."

"How's that math coming?" asked the paper.

"Um, it's all right, I guess." My daughter was a million miles away. She was concentrating so hard on what lay ahead, she'd forgotten where she was. "How's work?"

That brought the paper down. "Fine." He glanced at her sitting in the chair, confirmed it was his daughter, and resumed the position.

It took her a long time to get it out. I think if she had known I was there, she might have had an easier time, but she thought she was alone. Finally, she spoke, "Daddy, can I . . . um . . . talk to you?"

"Uh, huh." The paper never moved.

"See, I, um . . ." The tears came again.

The paper was quicker. "How much do you need?"

It was probably the one time in her life it did not give her pleasure to say, "I don't need any money, Dad."

Again came the glance to make sure it wasn't someone else's daughter sitting opposite him.

"I . . . when . . . See, last . . ."

"Have you done something wrong?" I don't think he knew she was crying. Even he could not be that insensitive.

"Sort of." She paused to tell the truth. "Yes."

"What is it this time, Sarah? Somehow you always manage to get yourself into these messes, and you expect me to get you out." Although his words were true, he was missing her spirit. She was so open to him, and he was launching into lecture number 102 on Being Prepared. "Do you need to use the computer at the office again?"

"No, Dad!" she practically screamed at him.

"Then what is it?" He saw her face for the first time. He saw her red puffy eyes, he saw her disheveled clothes, and most of all, he saw her fear. "What is it?"

She dropped her head.

"It can't be that bad. It never is." He paused and adjusted his paper. "Well, I can't help you if you won't talk to me."

"I'm trying." She was crying in heaving sobs.

Dan was preparing his mind to accept a failing test grade. I could see him thinking, *Surely that's all it is.* I knew then that there was no way she could tell him. His spirit was communicating that he didn't want to know. "What is it?"

She shocked me badly when she said, "I'm leaving home."

I went straight to my bedroom. Sarah passed my room, went to hers, and slammed the door. That had not gone well. I braced for the aftershock.

"Beverly?" The paper called from the living room.

"I'm in here, Dan," I shouted from the bedroom.

He walked into our room. "What's going on with Sarah? She came in and announced that she was leaving home."

That wasn't quite the way it happened, but I held my tongue.

"What's going on? Do you know something about this?"

"Sarah's pregnant, Dan." *Take deep breaths.*

"She's . . . what?"

"Sarah is pregnant."

I watched the tidal wave of emotion crash down on my husband. He was drowning and there was nothing to hold onto. I knew how he felt, I was only one hour removed from it myself. He grabbed for the first thing he could think of. He sputtered and choked out, "Is this that boy she went to the dance with?"

I nodded.

"I told you I didn't want her going to the dance with him."

I could see it coming a mile away, but it didn't make it any easier when he said, "How could you let this happen?"

"How could *I* let this happen? Are you saying this is my fault?"

"You don't keep up with what's going on with her!" He was screaming at me.

"*I* don't keep up with what's going on with her?" I was enraged. "You don't manage to make it home before eight o'clock one night of the week, you don't go to church with us anymore, and you're keeping up a little better? I don't think so!" The fire between us was raging, and I had just poured gasoline on it.

"I'm just trying to provide a living for my family!" he spat. "I guess I'll have to do a little better around here!"

I helped him condemn himself. "Yeah,. well, we would appreciate it."

He took the offensive again. "I don't think you realize how this is going to affect us."

"And how is this going to affect us?"

"I'm a deacon, for crying out loud! What am I going to say about this?" He was breathing very hard. "And what about you? You know how your friends talk. They talk when there's nothing to talk about!"

"So that's it." I said it quietly. Finally we got to the heart of it. "Our reputation in this community is more important to you than our own daughter?"

"That is not what this is about!"

"That *is* what this is about, and you know it!"

"Yeah? Well, she made her bed. . . ."

"Don't finish that," I warned. "It's hard enough for her to talk to you as it is."

"Why is it so hard?"

He knew it was true; he just didn't know what to do about it. I decided to give him a clue. "Why is it so hard? Maybe because you never talk to her? Maybe because you never look at her? Maybe because you never put that paper down long enough to realize that you have a daughter who needs you very much? Maybe more now than she ever has."

"That's not fair, Beverly. Sarah has made a very wrong choice."

"I know that! And don't you think *she* knows that? What are you going to do? Ground her? She's only fifteen. She's still our little girl." It was my turn to cry, and I did. "She's never had a job, never been to the prom, never driven a car." I wept for my daughter and the consequences she would live with for the rest of her life. I said softly to my husband, "I believe the only question we have to answer is Will she be better off with our love and support, or without it?"

I think it took him some time to answer that question. But he did. For an hour and a half he wrestled with his pride, with his emotions, with his reputation, and I believe, with his God. Because the man who walked out of our bedroom to knock on the door of our little girl's room was not the same man who had walked in.

"Knock, knock." He stood at her door and tapped his knuckles lightly near the sign that said, "Sarah's Mess." He tried the door and it opened.

"Go away," came her reply.

He stood in the doorway. "Sarah. . . ."

"Daddy, I really don't feel like talking right now." She had her back to him.

"Listen, Sarah, your mother and I were just talking. . . ."

"I could hear you."

"I guess you could," he realized sadly.

"You can say I told you so." Sarah was crying again. "You can say you were right. Because you *were* right, and I was wrong."

"That's not what I came here to say," he insisted.

"Yeah, well, you were right."

"Sometimes it hurts to be right." He was telling the truth. He would much rather have been wrong about Cody.

"I wouldn't know. Sometimes it hurts to be alive." She, too, was telling the truth. She went to her closet to get her shoes.

"Sarah, what are you doing?"

"Packing."

He was dumbfounded. I don't think it ever crossed his mind that she was serious, and that she would actually leave. "Where are you going?"

"I don't know yet."

"You can't go." He tried to sound authoritative, but he knew he couldn't really stop her. But what he said next did stop her. "I don't want you to go." Sarah stopped packing and looked at her daddy. But he didn't see her. He had picked up her doll, Baby. "You're just my little girl. I remember when you used to play with Baby downstairs on the living room floor." He was staring at the doll like he could see through it. "I'd be reading my paper and you'd come over to me. Remember our game? You'd knock on the paper and you'd look up at me with your big blue eyes and you'd whisper to me. . . ."

Sarah was there, right beside him, whispering, "Daddy? Will you hold Baby?"

My husband wept. He held Sarah with all the strength he had. "I love you, Sarah."

"Do you, Dad?"

"More than anything," he whispered to her. "I let other things take me away. Please forgive me. I was so foolish. Please forgive me. Don't go away."

"But I'm going to have a baby."

And I heard my husband say, "Your mother

and I are gonna be right there with you." Tears were pouring out of my eyes.

"What will people say?" Sarah could barely squeak out the words.

He paused, swallowed hard, and gave her the answer that got us through the next year. "I hope they say I make a terrific grandpa."

They did say that, and they still do. Our granddaughter is five years old today. Sarah named her Grace, and we all agreed it was the very best name. For not since Jesus was born in the manger has a baby brought one family such awareness of their sin and such rejoicing over their forgiveness. The concept of God's unfailing grace is not a mere topic around our house; it is our way of life. Little Grace ushered it in.

If you would like to have Paul and Nicole Johnson perform at your church, conference, or special event, please call or write:

interAct Speaker's Bureau
8012 Brooks Chapel Road, Suite 243
Brentwood, TN 37027
(800) 370-9932

The stories contained in this book are also available as scripts for dramatic presentations. For further information, write:

Paul and Nicole Johnson
254 Glenstone Circle
Brentwood, TN 37027
(615) 377-0093